Community

Gardens

PENNY WOODWARD has a Bachelor of Science in Botany and Zoology. She began her gardening career working as a volunteer at the Chelsea Physic Garden in London. On her return to Australia she worked at the National Trust Property Mooramong, and later established her own successful herb garden and nursery. She now works as a freelance writer and photographer and has published five best-selling gardening books.

Penny's articles and photographs are published in magazines and newspapers and she appears as an expert panellist on gardening talk-back programs. She is a member of the Herb Society of Victoria, Friends of the Royal Botanic Gardens Melbourne, the Australian Garden History Society and the Horticultural Media Association (Vic.). In her spare time she reads and goes for long walks along deserted beaches.

PAM VARDY graduated as a teacher but currently works part-time as practice manager for her husband in his solo medical practice. She has been involved in radio for nearly three decades through Community Radio 3CR Melbourne. During this time she has had many roles but is currently the co-ordinator, panel operator and weekly presenter of the 3CR Gardening Show. Pam is a member of the Executive Committee of the Horticultural Media Association (Vic.) and chairperson of the Management Committee of Cultivating Community – a not-for-profit organization managing the community gardens on public housing estates. She is a very keen home cook and is also a member of the Slow Food International Association.

PENNY WOODWARD AND PAM VARDY

Community Gardens

A CELEBRATION OF
THE PEOPLE, RECIPES
AND PLANTS

HYLAND HOUSE

DEDICATIONS

Pam
In memory of Poppa who was always so proud of my achievements.

Penny
For Ellen and Dan who represent the future of our diverse and vibrant country.

First published in Australia in 2005 by
Hyland House Publishing Pty Ltd
PO Box 122
Flemington
Victoria 3031

National Library of Australia
Cataloguing-in-publication data:

Woodward, Penny.
Community gardens : a celebration of the people, recipes and
plants.

Bibliography.
Includes index.
ISBN 1 86447 096 8.

1. Community gardens - Australia. 2. Gardeners - Australia -
Interviews. 3. Recipes - Australia. I. Vardy, Pam. II.
Title.

635.0994

Edited by Nerissa Greenfield
Layout and Design by Rob Cowpe Design
Printed by Everbest, China

Contents

Foreword by Stephanie Alexander

THIS IS AN INSPIRING AND UPLIFTING BOOK. I had no idea that there were as many as 650 community garden plots in inner Melbourne, cared for by a very wide range of dedicated gardeners, all residents of public housing estates, representing many different nationalities and cultural groups. The authors have interviewed many of these people and their stories are very moving. We read of displacement due to war or civil conflict, of broken families, of separations from parents or children, of isolation. But we also read of the delight found in growing familiar foods, in finding new friends, in overcoming communication problems by means of a big smile or an exchange of plants. The garden plots and gardening are seen as 'something for the soul' as one woman states. They are an affirmation of identity and more simply a haven and sometimes a retreat.

The gardeners may have come from very varied cultures but what they share is a heritage that valued caring for a productive garden. They are overjoyed to have the opportunity to continue this activity in a new land in their everyday lives. Many have encouraged their children or grandchildren to become involved also. Most speak of their passion for organically-produced food crops, for saving their own seeds and their absolute belief in the power of fresh air and fresh food.

The first part of the book consists of the stories of the gardeners, originally from Africa, South-East Asia, Greece, China, South and Central America, Oceania, the Middle East, East Timor or Eastern Europe. The second part describes and identifies the plants grown, gives practical cultivation notes and suggests ways they may be used. Many of the plants will be unfamiliar to Anglo-Saxon readers and there is much to be learnt about aloe vera, epazote, bitter melon, orach, mallow, kale and taro to mention just a few. Not just in cooking dishes, but many of the plants are also valued for their therapeutic qualities.

I feel sure that these inspiring stories will lead to an even greater demand for community gardens, and to already existing home gardeners becoming a little more adventurous in what they grow and try.

Stephanie Alexander

Foreword by Peter Cundall

THERE'S NEVER, EVER BEEN A BOOK LIKE THIS. But never before have there been times like these, so it is a book that had to be written. Right now, even as the worst things are happening in the world, societies are tentatively approaching the edge of the best of times. In essence, that's what *Community Gardens* is really all about. Jointly authored by Penny Woodward and Pam Vardy, it brilliantly reflects and celebrates the positive effects of population changes that are now occurring so dramatically in Australia and other parts of the world.

For the first time in the history of the human race, people of all ethnic backgrounds, colours, religions and cultures are cautiously starting to mingle with each other. It had to happen. And Penny and Pam reveal how this natural, ancient combination of people and soil in community gardens can strip away superficial differences despite diverse backgrounds and cultures.

To visit any of these mostly inner-city gardens is a remarkable, inspiring experience. To see people from almost all ethnic backgrounds quietly and peacefully growing things together, exchanging ideas, tasting and experimenting with each other's food crops, talking quietly and even using sign language to communicate with each other is an enormously moving experience. Most inspiring of all is the overall happiness of these dedicated people of the soil and their unconcealed respect for each other.

This wonderful book gives us a deep insight into a kind of future for which the human race has always yearned. It is a world of peace, cooperation, understanding, trust and, above all, one totally devoid of any kind of discrimination or racism.

Community Gardens takes us by the hand and gently leads us into an exciting world where people are learning together in the most natural way of all, by growing and sharing things together. It proves beyond doubt that the most precious resources of any country are always the people and the soil.

Peter Cundall

Acknowledgments

We wish to extend a huge thank you to Basil Natoli who has been our inspiration and mentor and worked so hard to make this book happen. Thank you too, Ben Neil, Peta Christensen, Liz Moore, Robin Parker, Andrew Woods, and the management committee of Cultivating Community for your enthusiasm, support and friendship. Our sincere thanks also go to the many interpreters from Vits Language Link whose guidance and interest helped to create a relaxed, friendly atmosphere during interviews. Thanks also to Tim Tolhurst, Jan Bartlett and Denis West at 3CR Community Radio; to Dimitri Serghis and Richard Kean at the Department of Human Services; to Lisa Boyd and Anne Hicks at Seasol; and to Joyce Nicholson for your support and belief in the project. Many thanks to our colleagues on the 3CR Gardening Show from which this project arose. To our publisher Michael Schoo, who always believed in the project, thank you. To our families, a very special thank you, for your encouragement, enthusiasm, tolerance and support whenever we take on another crazy project, especially for taste testing all the recipes (Pam's family) and proof reading all the text over and over again (Penny's husband). Thank you also to Anne Godden, sadly no longer with us, who first thought this subject would make a marvellous book. Finally, our gratitude goes to all the gardeners who agreed to be interviewed and photographed, who gave up their time and shared their lives – and especially to those we interviewed but were not able to include in the book.

Introduction

OVER THE LAST DECADE a green and growing revolution has crept through the crowded, and at times alienating, inner-city regions of capital cities around Australia. This is especially true of Melbourne where the grounds of Melbourne's public housing estates have been dramatically changed by the establishment of many colourful and delightfully enticing community gardens. These provide a haven to hundreds of families from all corners of the world. The human face of these estates is represented by a rich blend of cultural groups and the gardens play a vital role in the social, physical and psychological well-being of these people. To people struggling to adjust to a new land and culture, having their own patch of ground where they can earth their hands and grow their own familiar food is hugely important. The success of these gardens has been achieved because of the dedication and hard work of many people, and it has happened in inner city regions where good news stories are not common.

Although this book is about the gardens in Melbourne, it could be about any inner-city region in Australia, and even in other parts of the world. People from similar backgrounds grow similar plants in community gardens in cities all over Australia.

How these gardens work

At present there are about 650 plots, each an average of 2 m by 3 m, distributed through eighteen gardens in different locations around inner Melbourne. Gardens range in size from 10 or 15 plots to larger gardens with more than 100 plots. They are made available to the tenants of public housing, mostly in high rise accommodation, for a small yearly fee. More gardens are being constructed as this is being written. Each garden reflects the distinctive make-up of their particular community, as the gardeners mainly grow the plants from their homelands. The enjoyment and pride felt by these communities is manifested in community celebrations and the cooking and sharing of culturally significant foods, irrespective of race, educational or social circumstances. For many gardeners their participation and involvement in the gardens is a stepping stone for them into the mainstream community.

The Department of Human Services, Client Services provide funds to Cultivating Community, a not-for-profit organisation whose aim is to promote and support the development of community garden projects and environmental activities. Cultivating Community has a broad volunteer base but also provides administration and paid garden support workers for each garden. These garden workers are exceptionally multi-skilled people with backgrounds in ecology, permaculture, horticulture, education, arts and social work and with a real commitment to the gardeners and to making the gardens work.

Ben Neil, Manager and Project Co-ordinator of Cultivating Community says, 'I want the gardens to function well and for people to get benefit from that space. The important thing is that they get in there, get their hands dirty and get to grow food. If that is happening then we are succeeding and everything else will follow on. Obviously the people have to feel safe and comfortable too. They all have an equal right to be there and enjoy that space.'

Most of the gardens now have compost bins, some also have worm farms and all work on organic principles. Gardeners recycle their kitchen scraps and garden waste to provide more nutrients for their plots. Cultivating Community runs regular workshops to demonstrate how to make the compost and worm farms work. It is an absolute joy to watch the garden workers demonstrating what can go in and what can't, to a mixed cultural group with interpreters translating everything into five or six different languages. It is real life theatre. The gardeners also often save their seed from year to year and workshops have been held to demonstrate how this is done. One garden with a large number of East Timorese gardeners saved seed from their traditional plants to send back to East Timor to help their homeland regrow their crops.

Most gardens now have a shelter and tables and chairs too, so that people have a place to sit and chat, share a cuppa and a story. Cultivating Community also organises barbecues, festivals and bus trips to other gardens for the gardeners. These allow the gardeners to make new friends, to swap plants, seeds and advice and, as interpreters are usually present, to find a voice to discuss problems or ideas with people from other language groups.

Language can be a problem for the garden workers too but they generally manage to communicate with hand signals and by acting, by consulting other gardeners with a bit more English and, for bigger events, by employing interpreters. Peta Christensen looks after one garden where the gardeners are mainly Spanish or Chinese speakers. She is learning Spanish so she can talk more readily to some of the gardeners. 'This funny thing has happened: The Chinese gardeners, they speak to me in Spanish because I don't speak Chinese, and their pidgin Spanish is better than their English after so much contact with Spanish-speaking gardeners.'

The gardeners and their gardens

The people in the community gardens come from all over the world and the plants they grow reflect those they grew in their homeland. The gardens are full of unusual plants that are essential to the cuisines of the different cultures, as well as plants used in medicine and religious ceremonies. The diversity is fascinating – it's like another world. There is enormous potential to enrich the cooking and gardening of more traditional Australians, and thus for our culture to be enriched, by increasing our awareness of the diversity present in these other cultures.

Basil Natoli, Manager of Community Gardens Projects for the Department of Human Services, Tenancy Services, is in large part responsible for the success of these gardens today. He has devoted many years of his life, in both paid and unpaid work, to making sure that they continue to function and grow. He captures beautifully one recent visit to a garden: 'I see joy and a real sense of satisfaction in the smiling faces of the older Vietnamese gardeners in Collingwood who arrived here in the late 1980s and have immersed their hands in the soil of this new country, literally claiming a stake to a little piece. Their faces shine with delight and absolute pride as they offer bunches of the freshest Vietnamese balm, perilla, Vietnamese mint and assorted salad greens to me when I visit the gardens. These meetings in the garden are magical and I can't help but feel richer and happier for being a witness to such precious moments.'

The gardeners have enormous enthusiasm and real pride in what they grow. The tiny plots are filled to overflowing; where they run out of space they grow things in boxes or add tripods, fences and even roofs to allow plants to grow up and over. Every inch has something planted in it. The gardens also bring neighbours together, helping to build a sense of community through shared work, organisation and co-operation. Produce is always shared; when there is abundance the extra goes to garden workers, fellow gardeners, friends and family. Three generations of families often work together in one plot with grandparents passing their traditional knowledge on to their children and grandchildren. Many of the gardeners are women. Their gardens provide an avenue of escape from their potentially isolating high-rise homes. Children play in the playground or sandpit, while their mothers garden and talk to others. The gardeners speak of the importance of these gardens in their lives and for some, particularly Ethiopian, Eritrean and Somalian women, they are places of refuge where they can be outside with their children and friends, while at the same time growing the familiar foods of their homelands. The Hmong women speak of their cultural attachment to the earth and the importance of growing and using their own herbs in different phases of their lives.

It is well recognised that social networks can act as a buffer between individuals and the general socio-economic, cultural and environmental conditions over which they have little control. Many gardeners indicate that the community gardens provide the opportunity for a network of friendships to be built, some of which have transcended language, social and cultural barriers. The feeling that you belong, that you have a valued place in the community and knowing that you have friendships and supportive social networks are important factors influencing mental health and well-being.

Difficulties along the way

The benefits of these gardens to the people who use them are self-evident, but it is not always smooth sailing. Many of the gardeners come from backgrounds of dislocation, conflict and war; some have psychological and physical problems. The gardens can be a haven but they can also be a source of conflict. These incidents are isolated and really it is surprising that they don't happen more often, given the potential for misunderstanding created by not speaking the same language. The garden support workers need really good conflict resolution skills as well as their other attributes. As Liz Moore puts it, 'We have to be social workers, mentors, friends and disputes regulators as well as gardeners,' but she adds that it's a very rewarding job.

Another problem has been theft. One year, Dolphin's corn was stripped from his plot just before he was going to harvest it and Geoffrey lost almost his whole crop of pumpkins. Greater security and locked gates helps but it will always be a problem, even though it doesn't happen very often. Garden worker, Andrew Woods says that the gardeners have to garden with the possibility of theft in the back of their minds; they have to accept the risk

The future

The people who work with the gardeners are seeking to foster more input by the gardeners in the garden management, more workshops and they want to see more self-sufficiency (two gardens already have chooks). Robin Parker, another garden worker, describes her wish list: 'There is so much potential. I think the gardens would be a great vehicle for training, everything from skill development around horticulture and permaculture, through to language and cooking. Also child care – there's lots of potential there. I'd like to see the gardens become a bit more enterprising, to actually formalise market days or swap meets. Finally I see the gardens as great places for preservation of everything from biodiversity in our vegetable collections through to language, heritage, culture and stories.'

Researching and writing

While researching this book, we spent uncounted wonderful hours talking to and photographing gardeners from many different ethnic and socio-economic back-grounds. Without exception, they treated us as friends and confidants and we experienced hours of fun, laughter, sadness and reflection. We felt especially privileged, because under normal circumstances we would not have been able to understand each other as most did not have a good command of English and we speak no other languages. With the help of interpreters we were able to step into the worlds of people with whom otherwise we might only have been able to share a smile. So often, mistrust between people from different cultures stems from an inability to speak the same language. We were lucky to have this barrier surmounted for us by the hardworking interpreters. In all we interviewed over seventy gardeners over many, many months.

The stories in this book represent the thoughts and short extracts from the lives of fifty-nine people from twenty-two different countries. As far as possible we have used the names that the gardeners asked us to use, mostly their first names. As most interviews were conducted through an interpreter, the words are often the interpreter's version of what the gardener was saying. This means that the language used in the book is a mixture of the gardener's, the interpreter's and ours. Sometimes we have altered words to arrive at a more standard, readable English, although we have tried to avoid using vocabulary that they would not have used. Our aim has always been to remain faithful to the rhythms of the voice and the story told. Difficulties of translation and culture have meant that in some cases there are gaps in people's stories, dates don't always make sense and not everyone wanted to tell us their age. If there was a reluctance to tell more, we did not push, especially when a partner or child had disappeared from their lives.

The interviews were in most cases many thousands of words longer than they actually appear in the book. Probably the most difficult task was deciding what to leave out and, in some cases, who to leave out. A very strict word count meant that not everyone we interviewed could be included in the book. Very early in the process it became obvious that every person interviewed really deserved a book devoted just to them. They had all suffered hardship, loneliness and death, as well as love, passion and joy. There is so much to learn and so much to admire.

The people we spoke to are the same as the rest of us, with families, loves, lives and dreams for the future. In this book we try to show the universality as well as the difference. And to do much of it from the shared perspectives of gardening and cooking.

Plants and recipes

The gardeners not only shared their life experiences but also told us all about their plants and gave us their treasured recipes. On some occasions we were invited into their homes to share a meal. There are more than ninety different edible plants described in the book and all of these are grown in the gardens. We tell you what they look like, how to grow them and how the gardeners use them. Where possible we have also included the gardeners' name for the plant. At the back of the book is a list of seed suppliers with details of some of the more unusual plants they stock. Nearly all of the plants described can be purchased as seeds or plants from these suppliers. A number of the plants described are actually weeds: nettles, dandelion, mallow, possibly a reflection of the need these people had, and still have, to use what is freely available and easy to grow. We were surprised at the extent to which gardeners use their plants for medicine. We should not have been so, however, given that more than 70 per cent of the world's population still depends on traditional herbal remedies and this herbal lore is passed down from one generation to the next. We have included a number of simple medicinal recipes as told to us by the gardeners.

There are also more than seventy recipes. They reflect simple, inexpensive, ethnic home-style cooking. Testing the recipes was quite a challenge. The ingredients were often hard to find and many of the gardeners had not included quantities. All the unusual ingredients included in the recipes can be purchased at Asian grocers, greengrocers, specialist delicatessens, inner-city markets and other specialty shops. The recipes in the book are based on those given by individual gardeners but sometimes they had to be adjusted to compensate for a lack of information or difficulties in finding ingredients. Recipes were tested several times until the right balance was found. We had great fun trying all the different textures and flavours and it gave us further insight into the lives and cultures of the gardeners. We very much hope you will also find them interesting and will share our feeling of culinary exploration and adventure. All recipes were tested using metric measurements with graduated measuring cups and spoons. All measures are level.

And finally

Community gardens can play a vital role in bringing individuals and communities together, especially in our rapidly changing world. Reconnecting with the natural environment and growing something of beauty, or something fresh and delicious for the kitchen table is fundamental to our existence as human beings and provides not only food for the table but also sustenance for the soul.

We feel privileged to have had the chance to meet and know the people in this book. The whole process has been one of the most memorable experiences of our lives. We hope that readers will share the joy we have found in this insight into the simple human stories, the shared aspirations for happy and healthy lives for themselves and their children and the cultural richness and diversity that these wonderful people have brought to our country.

Pherina's dance group entertains residents and gardeners.

the people

the people

Africa

The people from the northern parts of Africa, here represented by people from Eritrea, Ethiopia, Sudan, Egypt and Cape Verde, have a similar heritage of farming and growing crops to feed their families. Plants such as *molokhia* (devil's mallow), *bamia* (okra), *regla* or *baqla* (purslane), *khobaza* (mallow), *jiir jiir* (rocket), silver beet, chillies, basil and garlic are all grown by most of the gardeners. Mint is also essential, to make the mint tea that is drunk on every occasion. The exception is Dolphin, from the Cape Verde Islands, whose heritage is more influenced by the sea.

Ibrahim Nour

Ibrahim Nour

Ibrahim was born in Keren, Eritrea. 'It was very beautiful before the war with Ethiopia, rich with gardens and farms around the city. We were farmers and we used to plant with the seasons, all kinds of vegetables and we had all kinds of animals. All of the families were very, very busy working in the farms and taking care of the animals. Nobody was sitting down. It was a very rich place but now it is destroyed, finished. They concentrated their wars in this area. There were a lot of forest trees and now all of the trees are burnt. When the war came the families shattered, split every-where, some in America, some in Britain, some here and that was the situation.' In a voice of quiet acceptance, Ibrahim goes on to explain, 'We had a big family, six males and three females. I am the youngest. Lots of my brothers and sisters died in Eritrea. Some of them were killed or died during the war and the others are still there. I have not seen any of them since I came here.'

Ibrahim came to Australia in 1994. His wife and 4-year-old son came a year earlier. In Eritrea, Ibrahim worked in a secondary school, teaching Arabic and Islamic languages, and Arabic literature, but since arriving in Australia he has not been able to work in his profession because he doesn't know enough English. At present he works making boxes from recycled timbers but at the weekends he teaches up to seventy local children about the Arabic language. 'When you have a hobby you should make it progress everywhere. Sometimes by teaching, sometimes in the garden, sometimes as a carpenter. I'm busy, very busy. Human beings shouldn't sit down. We should try. Always try. We shouldn't waste time. This is life.' Ibrahim radiates a gentle strength of purpose as he expounds his philosophy. His son is now in high school. 'What he does after that depends on his marks and his skills. He likes school and is good. He likes maths.'

Ibrahim has many friends in the garden. With his kindly smile he explains that sometimes they can't understand each other but he says his friends are free to take whatever they like from his garden. 'Sometimes they have a party here in the garden and I enjoy that.' The staples of Ibrahim's garden are the same as those of most other people from his part of the world and in summer his garden is always bursting with plants. In winter he digs it over and fertilises with chicken manure, because he says it is very warm so it raises the temperature of the soil. In summer he adds cow manure.

Sitina Dirar and Aesha Abdalla

Sitina was born in Keren, Eritrea. Her parents had a farm where they grew broad beans, corn and sesame, and before Sitina was married she used to help them. 'I learnt to garden from my country.' Sitina's father had two wives; she is the only child of the first wife, and the second wife had three sons. 'Two of my brothers died and I don't know where the other is. We lived in a very small house with three bedrooms. We left it and just had to get out. Everything was burnt. All of the nature

Sitina Dirar and Aesha Abdalla with grandchildren

ERITREAN RECIPE FROM IBRAHIM
Zignee is a hot and spicy stew essential to traditional Eritrean cooking.

ZIGNEE

2 tablespoons oil
2 onions, finely chopped
4 cloves garlic, crushed
1 kg beef, diced
½ teaspoon freshly ground black pepper
1 teaspoon salt
½ teaspoon ground cumin
3 tablespoons *berbere* spice powder (see page 15)
2 x 425 gm tins chopped tomatoes with added tomato paste
2 tablespoons extra tomato paste
1 bunch fresh coriander, finely chopped

In a large pot, heat the oil and fry the onions and garlic for 2 minutes. Add the meat and brown on all sides. Add salt, pepper, cumin and *berbere* and stir through (do not let mix burn). Add the tinned, chopped tomatoes with tomato paste and the extra tomato paste, stir. Simmer very gently, uncovered, until thick and tender, approximately 50–60 minutes. Sprinkle with chopped coriander and serve with plain, cooked macaroni or rice. **Serves 4–6.**

there was burnt down.' In a matter-of-fact way Sitina encapsulates the years of struggle in a few haunting words, 'The Ethiopian people caused us a lot of trouble and half of the population of the city died. Half of us are dead. We were very, very tired and that is why we fled.' Sitina's husband was a public servant. Over the years she lost seven babies and after they had escaped to Sudan, her husband also died. Sadly she adds, 'I have two daughters here in Australia and a son in Sudan. He is a father and has kids, we applied for him to come here but he can't come.'

Aesha was born in Umm Hagar, Eritrea. She says that this is an agricultural area and her parents had farms. 'We were five sisters and one boy. Our house was a big place with a big yard. It had two bedrooms with a verandah in front of it. On the second side there was a store, on the third side the kitchen. And of course there was a big place for the guests because we used to have a lot of visitors. There were two big trees and we used them for shade and underneath we planted mint, corn, lemons and oranges. I helped my mother in the house when I was young and she used to teach us how to make embroidery.' Aesha was only thirteen when she married and moved to Keren to live with her in-laws. 'I had no children from my first marriage and he left me.' she calmly explains. 'I

went back to my parents and then got married again. I now have one daughter and three sons. One son and my daughter are in Australia. Thank God that they are good and that Australia is good to us. They come to see me every day and bring their kids.' Aesha's other sons are in Egypt. She also has three grandchildren who live with her. With deep regret Aesha explains, 'Their parents died when the Eritreans started fighting each other. They died in our country because of war. This fighting was why many Eritreans left the country, because they are from the other side. The children came out with me. If the young people go back there they will be killed. If the leader was a good person and governs the country properly then the people would go back.'

Aesha has had a garden since she came to Australia and with her expressive hands and smiling eyes she captures what it means to her to have a garden. 'To have a garden is to me as if it is a friend, I entertain her, she entertains me, we entertain each other. Whenever I have a lot of thinking I come down here just taking this one out, putting this plant here, just looking after it. Something to eat, something to take home.' Sitina has also had a garden for several years and Aesha and Sitina grow similar things and use them in the same ways, reflecting their shared cultural heritage.

Aesha's only regret is that the garden is not big enough to plant everything, but she likes the salad things best.

Both Aesha and Sitina are sorry that they have not been able to learn English, they are not eligible for free lessons because of their age. Aesha articulates their sadness, 'Because we are old women when we go to the market we see but we can't talk, we can't ask because we don't know the language. So we look at them and they look at us. We just wander and wander.'

Basra

Basra's children Latifa and Luqman

Basra was born in rural Ethiopia. Her parents had a large farm where they grew corn, sweet potatoes, tomatoes, sorghum and maize, both to feed themselves and to sell. There were eleven children in her family and Basra is in the middle. She had no schooling but stayed at home and helped in the garden and the house. She says that all her brothers and sisters helped. Basra came to Australia in 1992 and her brother, nephew and niece are here too. Although she was single when she first came, Basra met and married her husband on a visit back to her family and he then joined her in Australia.

Basra's eyes sparkle as she talks about the many friends she has in the garden, and you know that she is a warm and generous person even though her eyes are the only part you can see as the rest is swathed in a soft blue *hijab*. Her friends are mainly from Africa. 'People tend to cultivate different plants from their native culture but sometimes if you are interested, or there is something you want then we share.' Basra mainly grows traditional salad vegetables and chillies. The fruit and leaves of the chilli plant are essential to her cooking because, as Basra explains, she grew up in a hot and spicy culture. Basra did not want to be photographed but was happy for her beautiful children, Latifa and Luqman to be included.

Fatima Ibrahim

Fatima was born in Biokahraba, a small rural town in Ethiopia. Her parents had a farm where they grew oranges, mandarins and coffee to sell and vegetable and salad plants for the family. They also grew the grain (known as *teff*) used to make their traditional fermented flat-bread called *injera*. Fatima has ten siblings and she says that she went to school but left when she was eleven or twelve. 'We didn't work on the farm but we served the men, took tea, coffee and food and we looked after the house and the goats and cows.' She adds, 'The weather was beautiful, not too hot, not too cold, plenty of water for the farm.'

Soon after she left school, Fatima's whole family had to flee Ethiopia because of the war. They moved to Djibouti, a tiny country on the border of Ethiopia. Here Fatima worked cleaning houses for more than three years, and then with the help of the United Nations, she moved by herself to Cairo. She stayed there for more than a year, before coming to Australia at the age of twenty-two. 'My husband and I knew each other in Cairo but he came here independently and we met again. We now have five children, four girls and one boy, the boy is the oldest; he is fifteen.' Her broad smile warms her face with pride in her children. 'My children are happy here and they are enjoying school. At school they speak English, but at home we mostly speak our language. We try to speak Arabic too. My son wants to do engineering. My husband is a taxi driver, usually during the daytime. My mother is here in Australia and two sisters and one brother. The others are in America and one sister is still in Djbouti.' Fatima has not seen her sister in Djbouti since she left in 1986, but her family in America have been able to visit.

Fatima really enjoys her garden. 'It is very special to have a garden. It is a little bit of home, something like that. It means I can make a lot of dishes from my country. I have lots of friends in the garden and we share plants and seeds.' As well as the more traditional salad vegetables Fatima also grows *talatam* (rue), spring onions, coriander, *rafu* (Ethiopian cabbage) and *rashad* (cress).

Fatima Ibrahim

Tawfik Mohamme Yousuf

Tawfik was born in Harer, Ethiopia. He describes the countryside where he was born: 'It is very fertile, good for the production of coffee and other foods, a very good place. Sure, my family had a garden; we planted everything in our backyard. We were all gardeners, my four sisters and my brother. I am the eldest and I looked after my sisters and my brother.' Tawfik completed primary and secondary school in Harer and then moved to Addis Ababa where he graduated as a teacher. Tawfik then went back into the country where, in 1973, he established his own school. At one time it had as many as 1800 students. Later a military government took control in Ethiopia and nationalised commercial companies including schools. Tawfik, his wife and six children fled first to Djbouti and then Cairo. In 1989 they were sponsored by a church group to come to Australia. Tawfik has been back to Ethiopia a few times and with great relish describes one visit where he went to see his old school. 'I went past and knocked on the door and I said, "What is this school called?"

"It is named after a person called Tawfik, they say that he is in Australia, somewhere like that."

"Ah, it is very nice, why don't you name it another name?"

"No, everyone here knows it as Tawfik's school."

"But I am Tawfik!"

He is surprised and hugs me and says come on in, it is your school. It was very nice. The school is good and still very big.'

Soon after they arrived in Australia, Tawfik's wife died and he was left to bring up his six children on his own; the youngest was only four. 'I looked after them by myself, being father and mother. That is why they are hugging me and saying always you are there for us. I wish one day that their mother could see them because she suffered a lot. When we were refugees in Djbouti

Tawfik Mohamme Yousuf

and Cairo, she looked after the kids, going and looking for food.' Their children have all been very successful, graduating in medicine, engineering and accounting, with two still at home. Tawfik now has grandchildren whom he sees often. With his beaming smile he radiates unbounded enthusiasm for his family, the gardens and life in general. 'We helped to establish the garden here. When I was teaching, botany was my favourite subject. I have made many friends in the garden here. Language is not a barrier because English is a common language for all of us. Even though there are different cultures, country, colour or whatever, English brings us together to chat and be happy. We learn about the other cultures, especially the Cook Islands culture.' He laughs and explains he hasn't yet learnt how the Cook Islanders use their taro, adding 'It doesn't have fruit like a tomato.' Tawfik grows food from home but also corn, tomatoes, coriander, lettuces, beetroot and cucumber. 'I come down to the garden every day at seven o'clock, after the news ends, I never miss the news, I keep up with the current situation. Then I come back and water later, sometimes my friends will come down and we chat, talk and laugh. The children don't come down to the garden. They are too busy but they share the jobs around the house. They work hard.'

The following four recipes are all used to make a traditional Ethiopian *wat* (stew). This recipe uses chicken but other *wats* are made out of vegetables, lentils, peanuts, lamb and beef. All use the very hot and spicy *berbere* mix and *niter kebbeh* (spiced butter) and are served with the traditional bread, *injera*.

ETHIOPIAN RECIPES FROM TAWFIK

DORO WAT

4 tomatoes
3 tablespoons *niter kebbeh*
2 large onions, chopped
2 cloves garlic, crushed
1 teaspoon fresh ginger, grated
3½ tablespoons *berbere* powder
2 teaspoons oil
2 tablespoons tomato paste
1 cup water
2 tablespoons lemon juice
2 teaspoons salt
1 teaspoon freshly ground black pepper
1 kg chicken pieces
4 hard boiled eggs, peeled

Peel tomatoes by placing them in a bowl and pouring boiling water over the top. Let stand for 1 minute, drain, and the skin will peel off easily. Slice.

In a large non-stick pot, melt *niter kebbeh*, add onions, garlic and ginger and fry gently until soft. Place *berbere* spice mix and the oil into a cup, stir, add enough water to make it the consistency of tomato paste. Add this paste to the large pot and fry for further 2 minutes. Add tomatoes, tomato paste, water, lemon juice and salt and pepper. Bring to the boil, stirring, and add chicken pieces. Lower heat and simmer, uncovered, until chicken is cooked. Add the eggs and simmer a further 5 minutes. Serve with *injera*. **Serves 4.**

Berbere (Hot Spice Mix)

1 teaspoon ground cumin
½ teaspoon ground coriander
1 teaspoon ground ginger
1 teaspoon ground cardamom
1 teaspoon ground fenugreek
1 teaspoon ground turmeric
½ teaspoon ground nutmeg
1 teaspoon ground cinnamon
½ teaspoon ground cloves
3 teaspoons onion powder
1 teaspoon garlic powder
¼ teaspoon ground allspice
1¼ cups cayenne pepper
½ cup paprika
2 tablespoons salt
1 tablespoon freshly ground black pepper

Using a non-stick frypan, toast the first twelve spices over a low heat for 4–5 minutes, stirring, so they don't burn. Add the remaining four ingredients and toast for an extra 10 minutes, stirring well. Remove from heat, allow the mix to cool, and store in an airtight container.

Berbere spice mix can also be purchased from delicatessens.

Niter Kebbeh (Spiced Clarified Butter)

500 g unsalted butter
4 cloves garlic, crushed
4 tablespoons onions, chopped
2 teaspoons fresh ginger, grated
½ teaspoon ground turmeric
4 cardamom pods, crushed
1 cinnamon stick
2 whole cloves
⅛ teaspoon ground nutmeg
¼ teaspoon fenugreek seeds, crushed
1 teaspoon dried basil

Melt the butter in a saucepan and bring to the boil. When the surface is covered with foam, add the rest of the ingredients and lower heat to a simmer. Gently simmer, uncovered, for approximately 45–60 minutes until surface becomes transparent. Strain liquid through muslin into a heat-resistant container and discard the solids and spices.

Will keep for up to three months in the refrigerator in a tightly sealed jar.

Injera (Flat Bread)

2 cups self-raising flour
½ cup plain flour
½ teaspoon baking powder
1 cup soda water
2 cups water

In a bowl, combine flours and baking powder. Add soda water and water. Mix to form a smooth, fairly thin batter. Heat a large non-stick frying pan. When a drop of water bounces on the pan's surface, quickly pour in enough batter to cover the base of the pan. Swirl the pan so that the entire bottom is evenly coated. When the moisture has evaporated and small holes appear on the surface, remove the *injera*. It should be cooked only on one side and not too brown. Don't overcook or it will be too crisp.

Stack the *injera* one on top of the other as you cook, covering with a clean cloth to prevent drying out. Serve fresh and warm. **Serves 6–8**.

Injera is traditionally made with *teff* flour (*teff* is a grain grown in Ethiopia) and the mixture is left to ferment for three days. Unfortunately, *teff* flour is very difficult to obtain. The above recipe provides a close substitute in both taste and texture.

Assi Yovanovic

Assi was born in Egypt, in Alexandria, but came to Australia with her parents and two brothers when she was one. They all still live in Melbourne. She says that her parents are not gardeners, it was her brothers who first started gardening at their family home. She went to school until Year 11 and then worked in sales. Assi now has a husband and two children. When her daughter Lenin was born they were living in a house with a big back yard. Assi had a vegetable patch and Lenin came to really enjoy the garden. 'She loved it. We grew tomatoes, capsicum, corn, eggplants and herbs too. I love herbs for cooking, they are good for us and the flavours are great and they're yummy and fresh.'

Assi has lived in the flats and has had a garden plot for a few years. Both her children like to come and help. Pointing to her garden, Assi laughingly explains, 'We made a little sandpit and Angus played in it a little bit, but like all small children he really preferred just to wander around and play with dirt and stuff. So now I've changed my garden and made pathways, and put bricks in so he learns to walk on the pathways and not on the garden bed. I thought, he's with me every day I might as well incorporate him into it because I do want him to learn where vegies come from, how they grow, get a bit of a love for it, the same as my daughter.'

There is an abundance of vegetables in Assi's garden as well as herbs, many planted separately into tyres. The plants she grows reflect her Australian upbringing, with everything from tomatoes to silver beet, and herbs like aloe vera and basil. Assi takes her gardening seriously and really tries to keep everything organic. 'I've found that the mulch is really useful for keeping the moisture in the soil. I noticed from the summer to now that when I dug the soil to start the winter vegies, the soil was much richer and I guess it's putting food

into the soil, and keeping the weeds down. I'm digging the compost in with every seed I plant; I put that in first, so I haven't used any fertiliser this time. I'm starting everything from seed and I want to save my own seeds. I love my plot, it's like my backyard. We yack and have a laugh.' She grins and spreads her arms to encompass the whole garden – it is obviously a good place to be. Assi is also a tap dancer. She is the youngest of the group that meets in the community centre. The oldest is seventy-seven. They make their own costumes and do a concert at the end of the year. 'My son loves dancing now. When I was pregnant I only stopped tap dancing at about seven months.'

Assi Yovanovic with her daughter Lenin and son Angus

Kerama Mohamed

Kerama was born in Cairo, Egypt. She had a three-roomed flat and everything was fine. 'It's a bit overcrowded and some people are not well off but they are happy and they live their lives very well.' She adds, 'The children went to school there. There is a great deal of respect between the teachers and the students. Homework has to be done on a daily basis. If any child actually misbehaves or is rude to the teacher there is a physical punishment.'

In 1993, Kerama, her husband and their four children came to Australia, with some reluctance on Kerama's part. Unfortunately after a few years they separated. 'It was very hard being on my own with young children in a strange country. Every day I cried.' She shrugs and philosophically admits that things are better now. 'My son is working and he is living his own life. My eldest daughter is married, she has two girls and one baby.'

Kerama shows off her garden with great pride. 'I like having it. I have made friends in the garden, we manage to communicate. Everyone here tries to grow his or her favourite plants from home.' She says her friend Ibrahim helps her if she can't come to the garden, and she helps him in return. She grows the traditional plants from Northern Africa as well as carrots, cucumber, pumpkin, broccoli and broad beans. 'Yes the garden has helped me, the garden is my best friend. My friend the garden. I finish my work, I come to the garden, I water, I am happy.' When Kerama is not caring for her family or her garden she works as a volunteer at a nearby hospital.

Kerama Mohamed and grandchildren

Rawda Ibramim

Rawda Ibramim

Rawda was born in a small town in Sudan. There were ten children in her family. Her father farmed the land and after he died, the children took over. 'We had to walk far to get to the land. We waited for autumn to come for the rains, then we put the seeds in the soil and we would go there to irrigate it and clear the weeds and then we waited for them to be plants. We used to plant corn, different kinds of corn that we used for bread and to feed animals and to feed people.'

Her son came to Australia in 1996; he is a doctor with qualifications from a Sudanese university, but he has been working as a taxi driver and is hoping to pass the exam to allow him to practise in Australia. In 1998 Rawda came to Australia with her three daughters and another son. 'It was very difficult for us before and when we came here because my husband was missing, we didn't know where he was. Then when we applied for him to come the first time he was refused. The second time we spon-sored him and he was refused. For the third time I went to Cairo and I saw him there and I finished all the documents there and he was accepted and thank God he is here now.'

Rawda has had a garden for more than two years. 'I feel relaxed and settled when I come here and work. I have friends in the garden. All of my friends speak Arabic. Some speak English of course but I can't express myself very well in English. I ask my friends about their gardens because I don't have any idea about most of the vege-tables here. I followed their experience and their information.' Rawda says that now she is able to help others too and she shares seeds, plants and produce with the other gardeners.

Traditional food is still the order of the day in Rawda's home; her cooking has not changed much but she has learnt to use some new foods. 'Before coming here I didn't know about parsley, but now I put a bit of parsley with the food. Nowadays we use mint with food too.' In the past she only used mint to add it to tea. She smiles charmingly and explains, 'We drink it all day. If we are alone we drink it, if we have any visitors we drink it. The whole day we drink tea with mint.'

Rawda adjusts her beautiful red *hijab* and looks around the garden, explaining that on their farm they didn't use fertilisers. They would grow a crop, burn it after harvest and then leave that area to rest for a year. In her garden here, she adds compost but no other fertilisers. 'Nowadays everything

is fertilised without any taste. The old vegetables are tasty because they have their own time to grow and see the sun, to be ready to pick. I give my garden the time to grow up naturally. Every day I come to the garden and sometimes when I am passing here and see someone I know I come in and say hello. I really enjoy the garden. My children used to say that you are very tired, what are you doing in the garden, just sit down and relax.' Her mercurial smile reappears and she adds, 'But the garden rejuvenates me.'

Dolphin Travares

Dolphin Travares

Dolphin was born in Cape Verde Islands, on Santiago at Praia. He describes his home island as tropical, mountainous and very green with lots of rain. Dolphin's father was a nurse and his mother stayed home and looked after the children. He grins, showing his impish sense of humour, knowing he's going to surprise us. 'Altogether I had maybe thirty-five or more brothers or sisters. From my mother there were fifteen. My father had three or four other wives. I was born very close to the sea. That's why they called me Dolphin.'

His grandparents owned a boat that they used to catch tuna, so they ate a lot of tuna, also turtle, dolphin and moray eel. They'd cook them with *patioc* (cassava), sweet potatoes, spices and garlic. 'We eat every meat but most of all fish. Fish is the best.' Dolphin talks about how they would throw rocks at sharks so that they could keep fishing and how his uncle was eaten by a shark. 'You have to be careful, if you jump in the water – pffff.'

There were so many children that from a very young age, Dolphin lived with his grandmother, who spoiled him. He says he never liked school, as if you were naughty the teachers would bash you. The irrepressible grin appears again, 'They'd bash me all the time because I was very naughty. Sometimes they sent me to school but I didn't go, I go swimming. My grandma say don't go to school, so I no go to school. I was maybe fourteen.' Dolphin explains that his father was black and his mother was white. 'We have blacks and whites but it doesn't matter, white or black. We enjoy life together.'

From an early age Dolphin had a reputation for fighting. Initially he just won mangoes but later, after moving to the Netherlands in 1969 at the age of twenty-two, he started fighting professionally. He also found work on the ships and at Shell and Esso. He started boxing training in Rotterdam and then fought professionally in different parts of Europe. 'I made a lot of money but I spent it all too as I had three or four girlfriends to support.' He shrugs expressively as if to say 'That's life – no regrets.'

Dolphin was sponsored by his uncle to come to Australia. He is extremely fit and still exercises all the time. He tells us how he gets up between five and six, runs down from the ninth floor, does his breathing exercises, runs ten kilometres and then runs back up again. At this point Dolphin jumps up to show us the exercises he does every morning. 'You see in Africa the lions get up at 5 o'clock in the morning, every morning, because if you don't get up in the morning you can't eat.'

Paradoxically Dolphin's exuberant enthusiasm for life means that he is serious about exercise and good food. He keeps up with his boxing. 'Boxing is good for everyone. It is the best exercise for losing weight. I help a lot of people, those that smoke a lot, drink, they come to the gym and they quit. If we look after ourselves then we will have a long life. Don't smoke, don't drink, eat properly.' Dolphin also dances whenever he can. 'Every one in Cape Verde dances, we enjoy life. Here is a good country, the best country in the world but people not enjoy life, every body

look for money. Money not important, enjoy life!' Dolphin also plays the trumpet and clarinet. 'I am musical, if you sing I will pick up my trumpet and I will follow you straight away. I put the music on every single day. I cook with the music.'

Corn is Dolphin's main crop. 'This is different corn. The corn is different colours, it tastes better, stronger, very sweet but hot as well.' The corn that Dolphin grows has multicoloured kernels and more starch and less sugar than the sweet corns more commonly grown in Australia. He also grows pumpkins and broad beans. 'I have made friends with the other gardeners. I give them corn. Sometimes I water their gardens if they don't come for a couple of days.' Dolphin says that he never eats in a restaurant, he always cooks for himself. 'I eat my own food. I eat healthy food. I don't eat rubbish. I make a very special dish with the corn, from my country, called *cachupa*. You eat it in the morning, you stay all day and you no need to eat, it will keep you, you never become fat.' *Cachupa* is the national dish of Cape Verde, it represents home and is always cooked on special occasions.

Dolphin goes to church and says that the pastor likes him to come because he dances. 'They are very good people, from Malaysia, China, Indonesia. They pick me up, invite me to dinner, lunch. I will stay in Melbourne, I like living in the flats, now they are beautiful.

the people

South-East Asia

The gardeners from Vietnam and Laos have a similar heritage of disruption caused by war. They took whatever escape offered itself and families often ended up in different countries, thousands of kilometres apart. Relationships foundered when one partner made it to safety and years passed before the other could join them. Sometimes children also had to be left behind with grandparents or other relatives.

The plants grown were usually tropical in origin and the herbs and vegetables grown in Australia reflect the gardeners' countries of origin. The Vietnamese grow lettuce, bitter melon, *bau* (edible bottle gourd), aloe vera, spring onion, garlic, lemon grass, coriander, *can nuoc* (water celery), Chinese celery, *den* (amaranth), *tia to* (perilla), *dap ca* (fish plant), *rau ma* (gotu kola), *la cam* (purple rice plant), *xa lach xoong* (watercress), *ngo gai* (long-leafed coriander), beans, silver beet, mint, *tan* (five-seasons herb), *bac ha* (taro), *rau ram* (Vietnamese mint), *kinh gioi* (Vietnamese balm) and basil.

Mor Yang and Mai Xue Yang with their children Pashao. Peter and Aryuvang

Mai Xue Yang , Chue Lor and Mor Yang

Mai was born in Laos, but she is not sure where because they went to Thailand when she was four. 'I don't remember anything about Laos. My whole family went to Thailand. We have five children in the family. We were in a refugee camp in the northern part of Thailand called Ban Vinai.' This camp was home for thousands of Hmong refugees like Mai, who fled Laos when the communists took power. Mai and her family lived in the camp for about eight years. 'We were very poor so we didn't have any schooling. During the day our normal routine would be to get up in the morning and cook breakfast and then carry water to the house and look after all the younger brothers and sisters and also we did some embroidery. My mother taught me the embroidery. The camp was in an area surrounded by mountains.' Mai came to Australia with her whole family in 1989.

Chue is Mai's aunty, she was born in Sam Neua, Laos. 'It was on a very high mountain. We had a big farm and grew corn, rice, pumpkins, cucumbers, zucchini, beans, chilli, tomatoes – you name it. When I was five years old I started to work on the farm. I never went to school.' In 1981 Chue escaped from Laos to Thailand with her husband and 12-year-old daughter. 'My husband was shot down and killed while we were crossing the Mekong river. We went to live in the same camp as Mai and I came to Australia in 1983. My daughter went to America; she is now married with seven children. I went to America in the year 2000 to see my daughter.'

Mor was also born in Laos in a village high up in the mountains. 'My parents had a farm too, a big farm. It took the whole mountain, even two mountains. I can't remember how old I was when my family went to Thailand. In Laos I didn't go to school and we just worked on the land, we didn't know the date, the month, the year and I didn't know how old I was or my birthday. My whole family went to Thailand and we were in the Ban Vinai refugee camp with Mai and Chue.' Mor's siblings and parents now live in America. She failed the interview to go to America, so with her husband and children went to New Zealand instead. They later came to Australia and now have seven children. 'My eldest daughter is now married and has moved out, but the others are still with me. My husband is still learning English so he is not working yet. He is also interested in the garden and my children like to garden too.'

The Hmong women say that they come to the garden whenever they feel like it, sometimes two or three times a day. They have had some problems with their plants being stolen and say that they haven't really made friends in the garden because they don't speak the same language. They grow fairly similar things in their gardens. *Xua jua* (mustard greens), lemon grass, *xau*

Chue Lor

zu cai (coriander), shallots, lettuce, mint, Vietnamese mint, nightshade and a group of herbs that they call chicken soup herbs. These herbs include plants like the aniseed flavoured reed *pawj aaib* (Chinese sweet grass), *ko-taw os* (angelica) and *kuab plais taub* (sedum). Up to ten different herbs are combined with chicken soup and drunk by the mother for thirty days after the child is born. These gentle, kind women spend a lot of time showing us the plants and explaining their uses but the highlight of their day comes when we try to pronounce the Hmong names. There is great mirth at our halting efforts. Chue also shows us some of their traditional embroidery, *paj ntaub*. So fine and delicate, but depicting typically robust rural scenes and village life as it was lived in Laos. Activities like farming, harvesting rice and grinding corn are all shown. Some of their embroideries are also known as storycloths because they tell the stories of their lives, like their journey from Laos to Thailand in search of freedom.

Ha Tri Le

Tri was born in Bên Tre Province, south of Saigon in South Vietnam. His father was a primary school teacher at the local school. His mother made and sold fish paste to help the family's financial situation. At the back of their house on an acre of land the family grew bananas, coconuts, some vegetables and had a pond of about 400 square metres where they raised fish. Tri's father was the gardener, though during school holidays Tri would help by digging up the soil. Tri did well at school and after Year 9 went to Saigon where he studied accountancy. Tragedy struck when Tri was in Year 11, both his parents were killed by the French. This ended his dream of going to university as he had to leave school and support his younger brother and sister. Fortunately he found work as an accountant's assistant and later, after further study, worked as an accountant for thirty years.

Tri's son escaped from Vietnam to Australia in 1980 and then sponsored his father, mother and sister to join him. Tri arrived in Australia in 1986 and came straight to Melbourne. Both children are now married and Tri has six grandchildren altogether. He sees them often.

Tri is very enthusiastic about his garden and very happy to have it. He comes every day, has made many friends in the garden and has learnt much from other gardeners. In the first year, most of the plants were given to him by other people, but now he has learnt how to keep the seeds and plants for the next season. He even manages to give them to other people. With gentle courtesy, Tri explains how he has divided his plot into four parts so that it is easier to look after the plants. He grows different things in different parts. He has also installed an umbrella that he uses to shield himself and some more tender plants from the hot summer sun. With excellent English he shows us all the traditional plants that he grows, as well as tomatoes, broccoli, silver beet and bush and climbing beans.

Ha Tri Le

His vegetables are very important because, after recent bypass surgery, his doctor advised him to eat lots of fresh vegetables. His gravity dissolves into a grin as he touches his chest. 'Now my heart feels very good because of my activity and the vegetables. The garden is very good for me.' Tri collects leaves for mulch for his garden from nearby Melbourne College, he puts them in bags in his trolley and wheels them back to the garden; his friend Thiep does the same. Many of the gardeners help each other, but Tri does more than most, acting as an interpreter when asked; recently he looked after Thiep's garden for six months while she was in Vietnam.

Do Thi Mien

Do Thi Mien with grandchild

Mien was born in Haiphong province in North Vietnam. She remembers a small house with a roof made of leaves. Her mother and father planted and grew rice for their own use. After the rice was harvested, the leaves and stems were used to make and patch the roof. She adds, 'We had to do it very thick so that water would not come through and we had string to tie it up.' There were five children in Mien's family.

In 1954 they all moved south to escape the communist regime, Mien was about five years old. They went first to a refugee camp established by the South Vietnamese government in Vung Tau Province and later they were given land to start a new life. Here they grew rice and vegetables, kept chickens and pigs, and Mien started school. There was not much money, so she left school after grade five and, along with her brothers and sisters, helped her parents on their land.

When she was about twenty, Mien married a fisherman from a different village, and over the following years five children were born. Then, with the communists in charge and Vietnam facing major difficulties, Mien and her husband built their own boat and made their first attempt to escape with their five children – the youngest only eight months old. Her husband made it, but Mien and her children were arrested by the communist police and put into prison. Mien says that fortunately she was allowed to keep her children with her. They made two more escape attempts but each time were caught and sent back to prison. It was five years from when they first tried to escape to when her husband was finally able to sponsor them to come to Australia.

Mien shrugs resignedly and then returns to the present to tell us about her family now. 'Three of my children have families and two are still single. Four are working, they work just as ordinary workers. My husband and I are separated and he has his own business. The children see both of us regularly.'

Mien's face lightens into a warm smile as she talks of her garden. 'Whenever I'm worried or not happy I come down here and I feel happy when I see my small garden. There are four Vietnamese in this garden, the rest are Turkish and now we get on well together. When we first came here we didn't have such a good relationship with the Turkish people but gradually we exchanged seeds and vegetables from the garden and slowly we started to get on well with each other.'

In her two plots and one she shares with a friend, Mien grows all the traditional Vietnamese vegetables. She sows seeds densely into one area and then transplants into another bed. Mien makes tea from dried Vietnamese balm, perilla and basil and says this is good for her health.

So Duc Nguyen and Vu Thi Ruyet

So was born in North Vietnam in Haiphong (south-east of Hanoi). He went right through school and joined the army at the age of eighteen, fighting with the French. In 1954, after the fall of Dien Bien Phu, So left the army, went home and then escaped with many other refugees to Saigon. Just before escaping, So met and married his wife and between 1956 and 1974 they had nine sons. In 1980, So managed to escape from Vietnam to a refugee camp in Malaysia; from here he was sponsored by a charitable agency to come to Australia. Later, So sponsored his wife to come to Australia but she wasn't happy because the climate did not suit her health and she now lives permanently in Vietnam. However, all nine sons live in Australia.

'I very much like having a garden here. I'm getting old now so doing gardening is like doing exercise, very good for my health. I don't participate in the other activities, I prefer to stay home. I have made many friends in the garden, both English-speaking and my fellow country people. I can speak a little English and can understand a little.'

Ruyet and So garden together, sharing their produce.

Ruyet was also born in Haiphong, North Vietnam, the same place as So, but they did not know each other in Vietnam. She lived with her family in Haiphong until 1954 when they all moved to South Vietnam. Ruyet was seven and had six siblings. She remembers a small garden in Haiphong where they grew some vegetables and fruit including bananas. In Saigon they were initially supported by the South Vietnamese government who provided them with food and accommodation. Later her father got a job making furniture and supplying it to the French, while her mother looked after the family, the pigs and grew the vegetables. The vegetables were used by the family but the pigs were sold. Ruyet says they used to grow bananas and used the heart of the trunk, cooking it first, to feed the

So Duc Nguyen

Vu Thi Ruyet

pigs. She says, 'We chopped it, cooked it and combined it with rice and it was very healthy for the pigs; their meat was not smelly, it was perfect.'

Ruyet continued her schooling until she married at seventeen. Her husband was in the army and she followed him wherever he went. With gentle melancholy Ruyet continues, 'My husband died during the war, I was very sad, and my children were very young. The oldest was only fifteen and the youngest four. I supported them by going to a farm to buy produce that I took to the market to sell. I used that profit to support my children and myself and the same money to escape Vietnam. Apart from that I had some savings from when my husband was alive and that helped.' Ruyet and her children came to Australia in 1982. Her beautiful smile reanimates her face as she speaks of her children. They like living in Melbourne, all four now have their own families and good jobs.

So and Ruyet grow a wide range of common Vietnamese plants in their garden plots. One is devoted completely to *kinh gioi* (Vietnamese balm), and So is very proud of his *bau* (edible bottle gourd). They say that most Vietnamese vegetables are good; they are medicines and they usually eat them raw. So laughs and adds, 'Every meal we have salads, herbs, we mix them with lettuce or water celery.' You can see as he looks around the garden, that he would know how to make use of the whole garden, not just the plots they have, but after a pause he laughs again and adds, 'Everyone needs a garden so we have to share!'

Thi Phan Thai

Thi Phan Thai

Thai was born in Saigon, South Vietnam. She has one older sister. When Thai was young she lived with her parents in a two-storey house. She remembers that they were very keen gardeners, although her father was working very hard as an accountant, so her mother did most of the gardening. Thai went to high school and started work as a pharmacist's assistant at the age of nineteen. She says that the family lived well.

After the communists took power in South Vietnam, Thai was working for a drug company that had a community garden. Once a month two staff would go and live at the garden and maintain it. They had to bring their own food so they could survive for the month and then another two staff took over. At the end of the season all the produce would be collected and sold to the workers. Thai says that this is when she learned to garden.

Thai lived in Saigon until 1986 when, at the age of thirty-two, she escaped to a refugee camp and then to Australia. Her sister had arrived before her and sponsored her to come. Thai says, 'When my sister, her husband and children escaped they left one child behind. She was ten. They left her behind to live in the house so they could return there if the escape plan failed.' Thai explains that had the house been left vacant the police might have confiscated it. Once the family were safely out of the country, the 10-year-old lived with her grandmother and came to Australia two years later. Thai has no children but says that she often sees her sister's seven children.

This charming, gregarious woman says that her garden means a lot to her. 'When I plant something and it grows up or it has a flower or fruit I love the feeling. That is why I love this garden. I have many friends in the garden. I can manage the daily conversations so language is not a problem. I participate in the outings, the meetings and the barbecues. I come to the garden twice a day. After I get up I come down to the garden at about 7 am and in the afternoon or evening, at about 7 o'clock, I come here again.'

Thai loves her chillies, grows lots of them and uses them in fish sauce. 'They are very, very hot. I use the chillies in my meals or I give them to friends or relatives, whoever wants them.' She is also proud of her *la cam* (purple rice plant) that she uses in festive rice dishes and in particular she delights in her flowers, because of their scent and their looks, especially her lilies and marigolds.

Van Tai Khien

Van Tai Khien

Tai was born in the city of Thai Binh, North Vietnam. Tai's parents passed away when he was only two so he lived with his paternal grandfather and aunt. Gravely Tai tells us that he has had a lot of hardship. His grandfather was a herbalist who, although he did not grow his own herbs, had his own garden and grew vegetables: beans, chillies, Vietnamese balm, perilla and *ngai cuu* (mugwort). Tai adds that although his grandfather worked as a herbalist he mostly gave his services free of charge so he did not make much profit. Tai decided that he wanted to work at something where he could make some money.

Tai and his sister both went to school. At that time the French were ruling Vietnam, so Tai completed primary school and then went to Hanoi where he worked in the daytime and studied French at night. Later, because he could speak French, Tai gained a job at the university working as a photographer of microscopic material. He patiently explains that it was very specialised work and sometimes he would spend half a day on just one photo, of say a very small amount of blood on glass. Tai worked there for twenty-five years. He married and has five children and now six grandchildren.

The family split up when they escaped from Vietnam. Tai explains, 'We escaped from Vietnam at three different times. I escaped and arrived in Malaysia and went to France. My three boys, they escaped from Vietnam and went to Japan. My wife and one of my daughters escaped from Vietnam and later they went to Switzerland. Then an Australian Catholic helped my sons to settle in Australia. So when I was in France I wanted to be reunited with my family but according to Vietnamese culture the parents always want to be with their sons so that is why I left France to be with my sons in Australia. My wife joined us too but my daughter had learnt German and she wasn't confident with her English so she decided to stay there. I really want to go to visit her but I can't afford to.'

Tai has lots of friends in the gardens and adds that he likes his garden because it gives him something to do every day and if he wants something, like chillies, he can go to his garden and pick them fresh. He also harvests *ngai cuu* (mugwort) from his garden to treat his arthritis. His only regret is that his plot is small and he can't grow as much as he wants.

Thi Thiep Nguyen

Thi Thiep Nguyen

Thiep was born about 13 km away from the centre of Saigon, in Theip Binh Xa, Thu Duc district. Her parents and grandparents had about ten hectares and grew many different kinds of fruit, especially cumquats and lemons. Workers came and picked the fruit that was then put in a truck and taken to Saigon to be sold. There were seven children. Only her oldest brother worked on the farm, the rest of the children went to school.

When Thiep left school at about sixteen she learned sewing, initially working from home, but when she married they moved to Saigon and opened a shop. Thiep explains, 'There were two different shops we were running then. First the tailor shop, because my husband was a very good tailor. He made jackets and vests, and the other shop was sewing material. During the fighting in Saigon, our shops were burned so we moved and opened another shop where we made American army uniforms. Later my husband joined the South Vietnamese army and died on the battlefield. Our boy was only six and our girl two or three.' Thiep went to live with her parents and over the next nine years used her sewing skills to keep them fed.

In 1984 she managed to escape from Vietnam with her son and daughter and three nephews. They made it to a refugee camp in Indonesia where they stayed for a year and then her sister and brother, who were already in Australia, sponsored them all to come. Both of Thiep's children have now left home and she has one grandchild.

Thiep grows many different vegetables and says that it is very enjoyable to pick the fresh vegetables and serve them to her family. She is an elegant, upright woman with beautiful hands that she uses to add emphasis to her words. 'I have made many friends, this gentleman (Tri) helps me a lot and I feel very happy here. The people here are very kind, they have many different types of vegies and if I want to grow it they give it to me.' She looks closely at her overflowing plot crammed with Vietnamese vegetables. 'It is full, there is no space for me to grow anything else.' Thiep gently touches the soft leaves of one plant and tells us that *tan* (five-seasons herb) is probably her favourite, she adds it to sour fish soups and drinks a tea made from the leaves to treat a cough.

the people

Greece

The Greek gardeners are predominantly women and strong, warm, caring women at that. They take an active social role in the gardens and know what they like when it comes to growing food for their families. Their gardens are not just a hobby, they are essential to their day to day existence. Losing their gardens would be like losing a limb. They all grow tomatoes (usually several different types), eggplants, capsicums, zucchini, beans, silver beet, oregano, parsley, basil and *vleeta* (amaranth).

Georgia Tsipouras

Georgia Tsipouras

Georgia was born in Kórinthos on Peloponnisos, Greece. She is the oldest of five children. 'It was a very tough time for money. After the war my country was very poor, it was very hard for everybody and not easy to find jobs.' Georgia would go wild harvesting in the mountains, picking the thyme and oregano, making them into little bunches and selling them on the roadsides. 'My father was a delivery man, he had a small, three-wheeled truck and he delivered factory supplies to the shops.' She adds there were very few cars so he was often also the local taxi, ferrying suitcases and passengers between hotels and the railway station.

Her mother looked after the family, the house and the garden. 'We lived in a small house. My mother was the gardener but I helped her a lot. I learned and I liked it very much. My mother never bought from a shop. She grew everything the family needed.' Georgia also fondly remembers that her mother taught her to plant flowers with the vegetables to attract insects to the garden and says that they preserved and stored the vegetables for out of season use.

Georgia loved school but like so many older children had to leave to earn a living and help at home. She married a local man and came to Australia in 1970 with her husband and two children. A third child was born in Australia. 'To tell the truth I did not want to come to Australia, my ex-husband pushed me to come. Australia is a beautiful country but far away from my family. In Greece it was very hard to find a job.' Georgia has been in Australia now for more than thirty years and during that time has been back to Greece four times. Her mother and brothers and sisters are still alive and living in Greece. Philosophi-cally she continues, 'None of the others came to Australia. It was very hard when I separated with my husband but it is a long time ago. I brought up my three kids and I am proud of them. The children visit me often, but there are no grandchildren yet. No one is married.'

Georgia first had a garden plot many years ago but says it was not well organised and a lot of things were stolen. 'Now it is all organised. I love it because I get out from the house and I love the green and I love the organic vegetables and to see them grow. I don't use chemicals.' Georgia uses compost on her garden and grows her own seedlings, saving seed from year to year. 'I come to the garden every day, usually in the morning and in the night. Over two weeks I picked twenty kilos of tomatoes, you believe it or not!' Georgia's face is alight with remembered joy. Like her mother before her, she is an ardent gardener. If you can eat it, she will grow it. She proudly shows off her garden, talking quickly and moving rapidly from one plant to another. As well as tomatoes and other typically Greek vegetables, Georgia grows several different basils, leeks, celery, sage, onions, fennel, thyme, chicory, endive, orach, nettles and strawberries. Her special triumph is a striped purple and white eggplant that originated in her home village. 'I eat mostly vegetables, I don't like meat much. In win-tertime I have all the vegetables, different varieties of chicory and endive. I mix them up in the bowl. It is beautiful.' She also makes sauces and preserves for winter use, and drinks sage, fennel and basil teas to keep healthy.

Konstantina (Dina) Tsirigoti

Konstantina (Dina) Tsirigoti

Dina was born in Gastoúni near Amaliás on the western coast of Peloponnisos, Greece. She is the youngest of eight children. 'My family had a garden, they grew every-thing you could imagine: tomatoes, egg-plants, capsicum, potatoes, lemon tree, oranges, mandarins and other fruit. My mother always looked after the garden. I didn't have any idea.' Dina explains simply that she married when she was eighteen then separated at twenty-five. 'I was too young to get married.' She talks passion-ately about families today. 'There is no longer any respect for mothers or fathers from their children and people work too hard for their children. It's silly to work so

GREEK RECIPE FROM DINA
Moussaka

olive oil for frying
3 large eggplants, sliced ½ cm thick
4 zucchini, sliced ½ cm thick
3 onions, finely chopped
1 kg minced beef
2 whole cloves
2 teaspoons cinnamon
3 teaspoons salt
3 teaspoons freshly ground black pepper
6 fresh tomatoes, diced
4 large potatoes, scrubbed and sliced
2 tablespoons butter, melted

Cream Sauce
1 litre milk
1 teaspoon salt
4 tablespoons cornflour
6 eggs, beaten

Preheat oven to 400°F (200°C). In a large frying pan add 2 tablespoons olive oil. Lightly fry eggplant slices and zucchini slices on both sides until browned (may need to add more olive oil as you go). Remove and drain on absorbent paper.

Add a little more oil to the pan and fry onions until translucent. Add minced beef and brown, stirring constantly. Add cloves, cinnamon, salt and pepper and chopped tomatoes. Lower heat and simmer, uncovered, for approximately 20 minutes.

Cream Sauce
Warm the milk in a saucepan and add salt. Dissolve the cornflour in a small amount of water to make a smooth paste, then add a little bit more water to thin the mixture. Gradually pour into warm milk, stirring, until milk thickens. Take off the heat, cool a little, then add the beaten eggs.

Lightly oil a large, deep baking dish. Arrange half the potato slices on the base. Cover this with a layer of egg-plant slices, and then a layer of zucchini slices. Season lightly with salt and pepper. Repeat layers in the same order using remaining potato, eggplant, and zucchini. Season lightly with salt and pepper. Top with minced beef mixture. Finally, pour cream sauce over the top, pour melted butter over this and bake, uncovered, until cooked through (30–40 minutes). **Serves 6–8.**

hard to leave money for your children and even your grandchildren. Here everyone rushes, works too hard.' After a few moments of thought she adds wistfully, 'In my country they finish work and get dressed up and go out.'

Dina came to Australia by ship, arriving in 1969 when her daughter Katarina was thirteen. That same daughter finished high school, then did four years at university and is now a computer programmer with two children, both of whom are their grand-mother's pride and joy. 'The rest of my family are still back in Greece, in Athens. I have been back to visit three times. I went back to Greece to stay and stayed for one year but decided to come back. I'm very happy living in Melbourne, but sometimes I miss my country too. It's very hard for us with two countries.' Dina speaks English very well and says that she learnt it from watching television. She admits that she watches a lot of television and often has it on just for company.

Although Dina never helped her mother in the garden at home, she must have inherited her green genes because her garden is packed with produce. In her characteristically unassuming way Dina explains, 'I learned to garden from the other people in the garden. I've made lots of friends here. The garden workers, like Robin, showed me how to do the tomatoes, how to fix them.' Dina generally grows traditional Greek vegetables and uses them in her Greek recipes. 'I use oregano and parsley a lot. I like to get food fresh from the garden. It is tastier. I love cooking, I cook fresh food every day, things like moussaka and keftepes. I have my recipes in my mind. I'm very happy to have a garden. In the high rise it's too hard to stay in the flat all day. If you have a little garden it is good. Fresh air, fresh food, and I enjoy seeing how they grow. Just this week I cut one tomato, my first tomato.'

Maria Kabylakis

Maria was born in Northern Greece in the village of Piperia, in the prefecture of Pélla. 'My village was a very small village, about thirty-five houses, lots of trees. It was all surrounded by mountains, very beautiful, good people. My parents were farmers and they owned their own farm. Everyone helped out on the farm and in the garden, the whole family.' Maria explains that she was one of five children. Her family grew many vegetables but their main source of income was from the silk worms, fed by the mulberry trees grown on their farm. From the purchase of the eggs to the harvesting of the silk took forty days and during this time they moved out of their home so they could house and feed the worms. 'They had to have the proper temperature and the house would be nice and warm, they would also create mess and under the house we would light fires that gave off sulphur to fumigate and make sure there were no diseases. It was a very delicate exercise. We had other places to live because it was summer time and you could sleep out in the balcony or on the floor. The worms started from eggs, we would keep them warm under our armpits. When they hatched we would put them on a nice clean cloth and then collect some nice young mulberry leaves, cutting them very fine like salad and they would start slowly eating. The whole house was eventually filled with beds of silk worms.' Maria explains that the silk worms go through several stages. 'Then we could see that the worm was looking to find room to create its silk. So we would go to the mountains and collect ferns and the worms would start to climb on the ferns and create cocoons. We would take the silk to the city to sell and it would go to the factories to be made into cloth. Then we whitewashed the house.'

It was Maria's task, from the age of fourteen, to plough the soil with the bullocks. Any snakes that she turned up were killed with a prodding stick. 'I finished primary school, and I did go a little bit further but it was during the German occupation and my father would not send me to the city for more education. I also learnt the mandolin and I still play it.' Maria learnt dressmaking as a trade and she and her sisters worked from home making clothes and teaching cutting to other girls, in exchange for produce or two gold coins.

Maria met her husband John during the civil war, when all the villages were evacuated to protect them from the guerillas. 'When things calmed down the whole family went back to their village, to the house. But by then I had met John. We stayed engaged for two or three years because John wanted to build a house so we could get married. He did that and we got married in 1953. John was a tailor, he had a shop making suits, and I was helping as much as I could because I had children.'

Maria Kabylakis

Maria, John and their three children came to Australia intending to stay only five years; they have now been here for more than thirty-three years. Their three children are all settled and successful and they have nine grandchildren, aged from two to twenty-four, who often visit.

Apart from her family, Maria's garden is the centre of her world. 'When I see something that is growing and I take it in, I say this is mine, I did that with my own hands. And I will keep doing that as long as I can. My youngest son and my daughter love gardening too.' Maria grows all the traditional plants as well as broad beans, garlic, celery, aloe vera, corn, nettles, endive, spinach, leeks and broccoli. Maria points to the plot next to hers, 'This garden belongs to my neighbour. She is a very nice lady. The other people, I would love to speak to them and I do, but they don't know English, they are mainly Chinese people. I say good morning and they can't understand, but I can see their expression and they like me and I like them.'

Kyriakos and Sophie Dimitriadis with their son Theo

Sophie Dimitriadis

Sophie was born in Thessaloniki, Greece. She came to Australia in 1969 at the age of five. She says that her parents were farmers, things were not going well, so they decided to come here to give their family a future. Sophie was brought up and went to school here but in 1981 she went back to Greece for a holiday, met her 'beautiful' husband, got married and had her family. They lived in a village on a farm growing corn, peas and wheat. 'All that hard work, the kids were small and we were struggling a lot.' As the children grew, their teacher told Sophie that the children had no future in the village. 'The farming wasn't going well, so in the year of 2001, the whole family came back. It was a hard life; the hardest job you can do is being a farmer. But I was happily married and I had no problems. We came back for the children; they have a better future here. We are very happy, my husband has work, the kids are going well.' Sophie is absolutely devoted to her children and is a very social and gregarious person.

She also loves her garden and the good food it provides. 'The gardening I think it is a love of nature come out in you. If someone has a plot and has the time to work on it, I think they'd be crazy not to get fresh fruit and vegies out of their own garden.' Sophie and her husband grow many different vegetables and she says she couldn't manage without parsley, mint, celery, carrots and onions in particular because she does a lot of cooking and uses them fresh in her traditional recipes – soups, spaghetti, dolmades and stuffed vegetables. Sophie smiles and says, 'The kids are not interested yet. They are too busy doing other things.' After doing a course in office reception Sophie now feels more confident and is looking for part-time work. 'Part-time work is fine, but you need to be there for the kids. My mother used to say the younger they are, the smaller the problems, the bigger they are the bigger the problems. The kids are very happy here and every mother tries for the best for their children.'

Vicki Nikolopoulos

Vicki was born in 1930 in the village of Koukounara, on Peloponnisos, Greece. It was a farming area and both her parents worked on the farm. Vicki was the oldest of seven children and also had to work on the farm helping her parents. 'I started working on the farm at the age of ten; the other siblings were younger and so going to school.' They grew numerous different vegetables and grains to use at home, but also olives, sultanas and almonds to sell.

As soon as she could, Vicki moved to the town to avoid farm work, but she couldn't find other work and ended with a job on another farm. Here she met and married her husband. She was twenty at the time and over the following years they had four daughters. Vicki's brother lived in Australia and in 1970 sponsored Vicki and her family to come. Initially they shared a house with four other families, but soon after Vicki got work with Red Tulip and her husband found a job with Repco and they were able to rent a home of their own. Sadly Vicki's husband died six years ago but her garden has been some consolation. 'Having a garden is like heaven, very good, very happy. I have health problems but that doesn't matter in the garden. I get more life out of working in the garden. My children and grandchildren garden too.' Vicki is a consummate gardener and grows all the usual vegetables as well as many others like broad beans, *maratho* (fennel), sweet corn, nettles, Malabar spinach, potatoes, lettuce, poppies, dandelion, mint, broccoli and watermelons. With justifiable pride she surveys her packed vegetable plot and says, 'I like to have as great a variety as possible in my plot.'

Vicki Nikolopoulos

the people

South and Central America

These gardeners come mainly from Chile and El Salvador. Most came for political or economic reasons and just as gardening was a part of their day to day existence in their homeland, it is equally important here. The plants they grow are similar: lettuce, cucumbers, silver beet, tomatoes, cauliflower, broccoli, pepino, beans, garlic, spring onions, zucchini and chilli – generally very hot chilli. Herbs are also essential, both for medicine and in cooking. Some of the more commonly grown herbs are coriander, *cedron* (lemon verbena), *toronjil* (lemon balm), lemon grass, *rudz* (rue), parsley, *paico* (epazote), mint, aloe vera, basil, *llantén* (plantain) and oregano.

Agustin Vargas

Agustin was born and lived his first eight years in Valparaíso, Chile. He describes his birthplace as a picturesque port, surrounded by mountains. Fishing is important but mainly it is one of the biggest shipping ports in the Southern Pacific. Agustin's passion for his country of birth is palpable and his knowledge extensive. When asked about the climate he describes in great detail the extremes of climate, the deserts, mountains, volcanoes, rivers, the thousands of coastal islands and the icy parts closest to Antarctica. He then goes on to discuss Chile's major crops and exports: fruit like peaches, grapes, apples, oranges, kiwi fruit; flowers and wine to Europe; copper all over the world.

Agustin and his family moved to San Bernardo, thirty kilometres from the capital Santiago. He explains that when he was very little they were very poor; his father worked in a soap factory and his mother

Agustin Vargas

worked from home. He had two brothers and some stepbrothers. Like so many South Americans his descent is mixed. His mother was the daughter of a French sea captain while his grandmother came from the Chiloé area and was an Araucanian native. Agustin did all his schooling in San Bernardo and eventually graduated as a boilermaker. He explains that this time was very difficult because the family had no money and could barely even afford to pay for the bus to school. He frequently found himself walking the eighteen kilometres to and from school, to save money or because the bus driver wouldn't stop to pick him up because his fare was not worth it.

At twenty Agustin married. He had already been working for three years and he continued working as a contractor for the same company for the next fifteen. He did well in the company, reaching a high position. After further study he gained qualifications as a technical draughtsman. At the same time he became involved with socialism and when Pinochet took control in 1973, Agustin was investigated and he lost his job.

Agustin believes that he and his family were lucky because they were able to come to Australia. He was thirty-nine and had five children aged from four to eighteen. Once here he continued to study and work

but unfortunately his marriage broke up, so Agustin took work as a welder and boiler-maker with companies from Woolongong to Woomera, seeing much of Australia at the same time.

The extended family is still in Chile and Agustin has been back to visit several times but he says that he loves Australia, 'I have been an Australian citizen since the first chance that I had to become one. I have been naturalised for more than twenty-four years. I always try to respect the Australian law and don't abuse what they give me.'

Agustin is a gentle, quiet man but he has strong feelings about his garden. He likes to fence his plot, believing that it marks it as his. 'It makes it look better, nicer.' The garden is 'happiness' to Agustin, he comes every day and is always asking other people questions. He grows many herbs and vegetables as well as some lilies just because he loves the flowers. He also grows what he calls his special Chilean chilli – special because it has a very particular flavour. Agustin shares his seed with others and he is happy to share other plants and produce too, 'I am getting the parsley and I have told people that who-ever wants, they can take and plant them. Coriander the same, to eat, they are welcome because if God gave me something it was not to be egotistical.'

Julia Soto

Julia Soto

Julia was born in Chile in a suburb between Santiago and San Bernardo. Her father left when her mother was six months pregnant with Julia so her mother moved to the south of Chile to a farmhouse. Here she formed a relationship with a master carpenter and had two more children. When Julia was four her mother died of bronchial pneumonia leaving three children. Julia then went to live with her mother's sister and started work at the age of twelve. 'I had to really start earning my own livelihood because my aunt had other children. I became a

servant, looking after two children. They lived in Santiago and I went to their place. I lived there because I had to take the children to school. I worked very well and I really looked after myself very well until I got married because, since I was very little I had to fend for my self. I got married at sixteen and at seventeen I had my eldest daughter.' She laughs, with a marked gleam in her eye. 'You are going to die when you find out how many children I have. Twelve children!'

Julia learnt to farm from her husband. They grew beans, onions, maize and wheat at the big farm where they were employed but they were also allocated a small plot of land for themselves. When her husband went to care for their small plot Julia would take his lunch. It was a long walk; she would leave home at about eleven and get back about two. When her children were older they would take the lunch. Julia and her husband had twenty-eight years together but then he developed heart problems. They lost a child to diphtheria, then her husband died and then another child died. All within fourteen days. Julia was suddenly left with ten children and no means of support. For a year they survived on the food that was left in their plot of land, then the government gave her a pension and some assistance, but not very much. Julia's indomitable spirit has kept her going, she says it has been a very hard life but adds with a chuckle, 'Now I am in glory here. Thanks to Australia I am extremely happy.'

Julia explains that it was only her eldest child, a girl who is now in Australia, who managed to get any sort of schooling, the rest had to get jobs at a young age. She has six children still in Chile. Julia came to Australia to be with her daughter but says the decision wasn't easy. 'It was hard to leave the other children behind but they are very happy that I am here because they know that I am fine. It is really marvellous, the flat that I have now. Australia has given me all the happiness in my life. I don't know how to thank Australia.'

Julia has had a garden since the year after she arrived in Australia. She is also a member of two clubs for elderly people. They get together for meetings, lunches, outings and holidays. Apart from that she spends her time with family and friends. She comes to the garden two or three days a week and has lots of friends here. She explains, 'I think almost all of us know each other. We get together here. Ladies and men. We try to help each other. We share plants and seeds. There is a Timorese lady and she shares things with us too. We live in unison here very nicely.'

In her garden Julia grows vegetables as well as flowers and has a camellia, roses and a peach tree. She also grows many herbs that she uses in cooking and as medicines. These include aloe vera, three different mints, *toronjil* (lemon balm), basil, *paico* (epazote), *borraja* (borage), *toronjil cuyano* (horehound), *ajenjo* (wormwood), *llantén* (plantain) and oregano. She believes that if you use the little plots properly you can really get a lot out of them.

Heriberto Urbino

Heriberto Urbino

Heriberto was born in Valparaiso, Chile. His father was a travelling businessman and his mother worked at home. They lived at the foot of the mountains and Heriberto says they had a garden which his father looked after and grew strawberries, peaches, tomatoes, lettuce and red and green beans. Heriberto went right through school to a technical school where he learnt mechanics and welding and later worked in these fields. At the age of twenty-two he married and came to Australia. His wife Maria joined him two years later. Heriberto also brought his mother and father to Australia and several of his siblings live here too.

Heriberto has had his garden for about eight years and originally got the plot so that his children could have some contact with the earth. With a touch of melancholy he explains that back in Chile they used to live close to the soil and it was very

healthy for them. 'Here the children are getting used to concrete, to everything very flat.' Heriberto grows things that he grew back home, that he saw his father grow. He has made friends with the other Spanish speakers in the garden and says he has learnt about plants as he goes along. He loves to experiment and try to grow things out of season. He is growing a Chilean papaya tree, but only has room for one, and a peach tree. He hopes that his vegetables will learn to adapt to different climates and seasons, in the same way he has.

Only natural products are allowed in Heriberto's garden. Everything has to be organic because the children eat the produce. Heriberto is relaxed about his garden but has very definite views about bringing up his children. 'What I tell them is that they have to study and then if they choose a profession we will help them along but if they want the freedom of the street then the door is there. That's what I was told when I was a child when I misbehaved, because I didn't want to wash my own clothes, they said the door is there. Back in Chile we didn't have all the things that they have here. We had to use our imagination. We used our ingenuity to make our own toys. If we wanted an apple we had to help the neighbour carry the bags. They don't know the effort to earn money, what one has to do to get ahead in life without having anything.' He goes on to say very firmly that he believes his children should be looking to their future and how they can help Australia.

Jesus Mazariego

Jesus was born in the Antiguo Cuzcatlan in El Salvador. She says that she lived in a humble kind of house but she doesn't remember much about it because they only lived there until she was seven. Her father worked on farms where he would do lots of jobs.

They moved to Tonacatepeque in the Department of San Salvador. Here her father worked as a *balsamero* – a person who gets balsam from trees by taking a machete and cutting the tree (El Salvador is the world's main source of the medicinal balsam extracted from the resin of balsam trees). Her mother worked making cigars: she was known as a *purera*. Jesus believes that there were nine children in her family but says that only three are left, the others she didn't really know because she was the youngest. She went to school for a while but when she was ten her mother died and Jesus went to live with an aunt. At the age of twelve Jesus went to work caring for two little girls, then after two years she moved to work behind the counter in a general store. It was a hard life but was helped by the fact that Jesus was able to stay in touch with her father and siblings as they lived nearby.

When she was about fifteen her uncle collected her and took her to another city, where she again worked in a shop. Jesus contemplates her life back then and decides it wasn't all bad. 'I was very keen and enjoyed working in the shop.' Her uncle had a large plot of land where he grew maize and beans and Jesus often went and

Jesus Mazariego

helped. This is where she first learnt how to garden and it is also where she met the father of her children. They continued to work on farms owned by her mother-in-law, mainly growing oranges to sell, and over the following years had nine children.

On the third of May 1965 their lives were literally shaken apart by an earthquake that struck at three in the morning. Their home was destroyed and, after living in temporary accommodation, they were eventually given some land and built a house. A few years later her husband disappeared and it was only years later that Jesus discovered he had started a relationship with another woman and moved to America.

One of Jesus' married daughters came

with her husband to Australia, and soon after they sponsored her to come too. Some of her other children are now in Australia and one is still in El Salvador. Jesus says that in El Salvador, even though the business with the guerillas is finished, life is still very precarious because of crime. She shakes her head in disgust. 'These days it is theft, they are killing people because of that.'

Jesus really likes having a garden but finds it hard sometimes because of her bad back. She has made many friends and manages to talk to the gardeners from other countries by using sign language. They manage to exchange seeds and plants, even if they can't exchange words. She is always busy. 'I sew when I'm not in the garden, I sew all my own clothes, just for myself.'

Marcos Lopez

Marcos was born in Las Canas, in the Department of Chalatenango, El Salvador. His father was a farmer and his mother looked after the children and the house. Marcos' father grew maize as the main crop as well as beans and pumpkins. Marcos says that they lived in a rural area and everybody farmed. His father had patches of land here and there and he tilled the soil with the aid of hired bullocks and a plough. Marcos had six siblings. 'The older brother did not come to school because he was helping my father. In general, the first one in the family is the one who carried the burden of the family.' The other children did help though, when they were not at school. Marcos remembers using a machete to help clear the weeds. At the age of seven Marcos and his brother had to walk the four kilometres to school. 'In winter when there was plenty of rain, the roads were very slippery, you were under the rain for a long time. I was on foot. Sometimes we had to wade, to cross a river.'

Marcos finished school and then moved to the nearby city of Chalatenango where he started work in an office. Later he worked registering births and deaths, then became an accounting assistant and eventually worked his way up to become the treasurer of the City Council in Chalatenango. He worked there for thirty years and only resigned a month before coming to Australia. Marcos is married and has four children. His wife still lives in El Salvador, as does one of his daughters and all his brothers

Marcos Lopez

and sisters. He came to Australia to be with his son, who is married with a child.

A dedicated gardener, Marcos says he has many friends in the garden but laughingly comments, 'These Chinese people, you don't always understand what they say but they are very kind people. I have a look at what they are growing, and they look at what we are growing and we share plants and seeds.' He is a gregarious, social person and comes to the gardens every day.

'You can go to the market and buy your things but if you come to the garden you get some exercise, you entertain yourself, you talk to a friend, it's an opportunity to do that.'

Marcos grows a lot of different vegetables but is growing a big crop of broad beans. He says that these were not grown in El Salvador, he has got to know of them through a Chilean friend and now really enjoys them.

Vilma Alvaringa

Vilma was born in 1952 in Suchitoto, in the Department of Cuscatlán in El Salvador. She grew up in an agricultural region on a small farm. They had milking cows and grew corn, beans, rice, tomatoes, pepino and cucumbers. When the seasons were good they would sell some of the produce but mostly it was used to feed the family. It was very much needed because she had fourteen brothers and sisters. Vilma attended school until the age of sixteen. She then went to the city to work, initially in a restaurant and later as a domestic for a consular family. She moved with them to Panama. When her contract expired she went to Mexico to live with a brother who was training for the priesthood (this brother was later killed in the civil war) and then back to Panama for three years working for the Swedish Consul. Finally Vilma returned to El Salvador and a year later she married a farmer. Soon after this the civil war started. Vilma's sister-in-law had moved to Australia and she sponsored Vilma and her family to come in 1988. Their daughter was seven and Vilma was seven months pregnant with their son. They all worked hard to learn English, her daughter picking it up quickly, but it was several years before she and her husband had learnt enough to gain work.

Vilma would like to go back and visit family in El Salvador but has used any extra money to help the extended family. Her father, still in El Salvador, has remarried and now has four more children. The eldest is training as a nurse and Vilma sends money to help her complete the course. A strong, independent woman with an infectious smile, Vilma speaks proudly of her daughter

Vilma Alvaringa

who works in a big employment company and her son who is in Year 10 and very good at maths.

Her garden is also central to her happiness. 'For me the garden is very important because I can plant herbs for medicine, vegetables, everything, and I have made many friends.' She grows many different herbs and vegetables and loves to grow flowers too, such as carnations and roses to put in the house. She calmly sums it up: 'When you are used to cultivating the land you want to have lots of things, because everything is good. You want to have medicinal herbs, food, everything you can grow.'

Alonzo Rivera

Alonzo Rivera

Alonzo was born in Buena Vista in the Department of Cuscatlán, El Salvador. He says that it was a rural area, there were farms and they worked the land growing maize, sugar cane, coffee and mangoes. It was very hot with six months of winter and six months of summer and lots of rain. He explains that the maize they grew was very tiny and white and they used it to make tortillas.

Alonzo's parents worked the land that they owned and this supported their eight children. They also had two or three cows, mainly for milking. Most of the children worked on the farm and although they went to school did not go much beyond fourth grade. At the age of fifteen, Alonzo left home and went to the capital where for thirteen years he worked as a waiter. Although he never married, he does have a son. His son's mother died many years ago. When he had to leave his country because of the war, Alonzo came to Australia with his son, his son's wife and his grandson. All his brothers and sisters are still in El Salvador and he has never been able to return to visit them and doesn't know if some of them are dead or alive.

Alonzo has had a garden plot for many years and says that when he does certain things in the garden it reminds him of his childhood and youth. He comes every day and has made friends with other gardeners, especially Vilma because they speak the same language. Alonzo grows plants similar to those grown by the other gardeners from El Salvador. He also uses rue leaves to rub onto his body if there is any pain. 'You rub it there very hard, rub the leaves and juice comes out and you rub it around.' As well he adds fresh oregano to chutneys and boils a lemon grass stem and drinks the liquid to treat the symptoms of a cold.

the people

Oceania

T he gardens of those born in Australia reflect the cultural mix that Australia has become. As well as growing the more traditional vegetables they have also watched what other gardeners grow and are happy to swap advice and seeds. Pherina has lived most of her life in New Zealand and Australia but her garden strongly reflects her cultural origins and is usually full of taro.

Corey Rawlings

Corey Rawlings

Corey is twelve turning thirteen. He is in Year 7 and says that he likes school – maths is his favourite subject. He also loves to play golf. 'I have been playing nearly a year and a half. I'm good at it.'

His family has only been in the flats for a short time and his mum Rebecca says, 'He wasn't too happy about moving into the flats but once he knew he could have a garden he was pretty happy.' Corey chips in and adds that when they lived in Melton he used to help his mum in the garden. 'We grew flowers. I helped with the weeding. I decided to get a plot here because I really like gardening and I wanted to grow some vegetables. I have learnt from my mum and from just putting them in. I talk to the other gardeners and I look at what they are growing.' Several of the adult gardeners have taken Corey under their wing, giving him plants and advice.

Corey has decorated his garden with small statues and he likes planting flowers amongst his vegetables. This year he's had a really good crop of sweet corn, lots and lots of parsley and plenty of tomatoes. He tries to be totally organic and has been

rewarded by finding ladybirds. Corey grins with pleasure and says he also likes to cook – he's learnt to make his own spaghetti sauce at school. He's not sure what he'll plant for winter, maybe potatoes but says he will talk to the other gardeners to see what they are planting and look at books in the library. 'I bring our compost down every day and put it in the compost bin. There was a whole heap of worms in the last compost and everyone was allowed to dig it out and put it in their gardens. Everyone came down and started putting it in their garden. So it was full and by the next morning it was empty. The next compost is going to be a big lot!'

Fiona Belbin

Fiona Belbin

Fiona was born in Melbourne and grew up in the outer suburbs, which were partly rural at that time. 'It was a normal suburban block, my mum wasn't much of a gardener. My dad was an architect but he died when I was very young. It was hard for my mum.'

Fiona says her interest in gardening probably developed in the 80s when she had a boyfriend who was crazy about cacti. 'That led me into a wider interest. In the beginning I mainly grew vegies and herbs and some unusual plants. Now living on the tenth floor you feel kind of detached from the world and you need to be grounded. I've made acquaintances in the garden, not so much friends but people you can say hello to. That's enough some days to lift you from feeling sorry for yourself and depressed, to feeling that life is ok after all. It doesn't take much but that little bit is really good.'

At one stage Fiona had nineteen different herbs and vegetables in her small plot and it is always overflowing with produce. She is patently a consummate gardener and seems almost rooted to the earth. Apart from the more common vegetables and herbs she also grows rue, fish plant, perilla, mallow, lemon grass, sorrel, dandelion, purslane, shallots and Vietnamese mint. 'I love eating and cooking, especially eating new things. I borrow books from the library, eat at friends' places and my flat mate is Iranian. That's where I get some ideas. My garden's always got stuff in all year round. I use mostly cow manure, twice a year, and I put on some of our free seaweed fertiliser. I collect grass clippings too. I would really like a composting system so I could use compost in my garden.'

Geoffrey Ward

Geoffrey Ward

Geoff was born in Walnut Creek, California. 'My mother comes from California and my father's from Melbourne but he was doing his post graduate studies at the University of California in Berkeley when they met.' Geoff did his first year of primary school in California but his father wanted to come back to Melbourne so they returned in the early 60s. 'My father was a really avid summer vegetable gardener. His favourites were all sorts of pumpkins, squash and zucchini. But we also grew sweet corn, because the kids really loved sweet corn, and sunflowers and silver beet, and tomatoes, things like that. Part of summer was gardening and enjoying eating the food that was produced. My father would build the soil up into a huge mound like a small volcano and hollow out the top and plant the seeds around the ridge at the top and then plants would grow out down the side and spread out. But to water it you'd just fill up the hole at the top of the volcano. So as kids when we went out to water it was like "Oh, I want to fill the volcano".'

Geoff went to Melbourne University but the taste of freedom made him realise that he wanted to do something different, so he dropped out, played in a band, read poetry and travelled a lot. Grinning ruefully at his younger self Geoff explains, 'That was a really good education and to see a bit of the world and find a bit of myself.' Later he went back to university, finished a politics degree and got a job in the public service in Veterans' Affairs. Geoff says he enjoyed working there and was also doing voluntary work when he had a bout of flu and just didn't recover.

He was eventually diagnosed with chronic fatigue syndrome and a very difficult time followed. Fatalistically he shrugs and explains. 'I've always been an optimistic person. Very positive mental attitude, always enjoyed life. You really learn to understand yourself, you have so much time alone just sitting there thinking. Just feeling exhausted and unable to do anything. You really want to get back to where you were and the old cliché that without your health you don't have much is really true. It's been a long, slow road. One of the things with chronic fatigue is that you get cut off from society because you can't work and you can't socialise much and you feel as if you've dropped out of the real world. Coming back into the garden has just been good, interacting with people again and getting a bit of confidence back.'

Geoff has grown tomatoes, pumpkins and squash so far. 'I'm pretty pleased with how it's going. I've just got into the garden for this summer's growing season. My partner did most of the hard digging.' They found that after clearing out a lot of rubble, the soil was quite good and they added mushroom compost and organic chicken fertiliser. His sister sent him some heirloom seed and he was given some tomato seedlings. 'We've learnt things from the gardeners who have been here longer than us; we interact with them, trade stories and ideas and meet people that you probably wouldn't otherwise meet.'

Geoff is optimistic about the future and is planning to expand his range of vegetables and include a few herbs. 'With chronic fatigue it makes me very wary of being exposed to chemicals and pesticides, so I grow without any of that sort of stuff and I'm very pleased that that seems to be the philosophy of most of the people here as well. I think the gardening has been really good for me, just interacting with people again.'

Mary Appleton

Mary Appleton

Mary was born in 1950 in Carlton and lived mostly with her grandmother before becoming a boarder at the convent school at the age of seven. 'I started being interested in gardening when I went to boarding school. They had a magnificent vegetable garden, beautiful garden – you could see it from The Boulevard. Rows and rows of vegetables, fruit trees, they had practically everything, they had their own farm, own bakehouse, own milk – everything. The kids would help to look after the vegetables, poultry and pigs. A couple of friends and I would go down with salt and pepper and pinch the tomatoes, they were so good.' Mary grins mischievously at the memory.

Mary left school at fourteen and went back home. 'My grandparents were living with us at that time. We had a vegetable garden and ducks and chooks. My grandmother and grandfather taught me how to garden because they came from a farm.' Mary's grandparents used to be part owners of Tongala Dairy.

Mary says that she has had a number of jobs. She also married. 'I had a very bad marriage because I got belted around a fair bit and I ended up in hospital. There was one bad time when I was living out in the streets, it was minus two degrees. So I had a pretty hard married life.' Her husband died and she moved into a flat where she was able to garden.

'I really like having the garden down here. The majority of my produce goes into salads. I have a lot of salads. Last year we had a bumper crop of tomatoes and this plot over here had potatoes, I think I got about ten kilos.' Her companions are her cats. Mary's first cat died and is buried in her garden plot. She proudly lifts one of the cats, stroking it gently. 'This is my latest cat, I just named him Woodside James and this is Sheloa Jessica and then there is Bubby Cat. My cats are never any trouble.' Mary also plays lawn bowls and has won trophies while her other hobby is collecting Golden Books.

Roy McDougall

Roy was born and raised in Collingwood. 'There was dad and mum and three boys and a girl. I'm the eldest. Dad had a barber shop and mum died when we were young – I was only about seven or eight. Dad carried on the barber shop and raised us on his own. I used to be the one that looked after my brothers and sister. I took over and got them and myself to school. We did it the hard way.'

Roy remembers that they had a garden and that mostly he looked after it. Apart from feeding themselves they would sometimes sell their produce to bring in a little extra money. Roy came up with another way to earn a little extra cash. 'Dr Mannix (the Catholic Archbishop of Melbourne) used to walk to St Pats every morning from Raheen, often getting a haircut on the way. He used to pay my father double for his haircut. I'd get up all the grey haired locks of Dr Mannix's hair and put it in a matchbox and sell it for sixpence a box over at the school. That way we got our lolly money.' Roy says that life was always a struggle when he was young.

Once he got his Merit grade he joined the workforce where he had a go at everything. 'Then the war came and it nearly broke me father's heart, but off I went.' Soon after returning from the war he married and had children. 'They're all grown up now and have families. So everything turned out for the best.' Roy moved into

Roy McDougall

his unit in 1991. He is a vital cog in his community, helping people in all sorts of ways, from filling in forms to settling arguments in the garden. 'Yeah, I'm happy living here and I think I must be the fittest one around here, from what I do every day, but I don't mind doing it.' In 1998 he was given the Australia Day award for Citizen of the Year in the City of Yarra and he has received numerous other awards for helping in the community.

Roy helped to establish the community garden near his unit. He didn't want to grow vegetables but a small area in the middle has been set aside for him to grow flowers. Wagging his finger at us with a big grin he warns – 'Wait till I put my garden in the middle of it – I'll liven it up! There are Turks, Chinese, Vietnamese, Maltese – four or five nationalities at least. They've got used to my signals.' There were some conflicts in the garden and Roy stepped in to help. 'With this garden I'm putting out here I'll help them all, spend a bit more time with them, and I can figure out their arguments and that. There's been some shocking arguments; I'm the public relations officer.'

Roy plays a similar role at his bowling club. 'I'm the players' representative. I stop a lot of arguments. Tell em to read the rules.' Roy thinks that the community garden has taken a lot of pressure off, that it's a brilliant idea and they should be everywhere. 'They get bound to their flats all the time, there's no yard or anything, and that causes crime. They're fighting with their neighbours and they're cramped up inside four walls. It's all right to say they've got a park down there – well, they sit and watch the kids play, I suppose – but that's not giving them anything to do. The garden makes them happy. I see them here in the garden at 11 o'clock at night. They're out here all hours of the night; So's here at five o'clock in the morning. These tables and chairs are used a lot, especially at night in the hot weather. Last night they were all sitting out here. The kids were all around, attracted to the apricots. Now the peaches are coming on. I reckon we can make this the best community garden in Melbourne. They're all trusting one another now.'

Pherina Tuaiti

Pherina Tuaiti

Pherina was born in the Cook Islands on the main island, Rarotonga. 'My whole family moved to New Zealand when I was eight years old. There are nine in the family, two boys and seven girls. My mum and dad were separated so I didn't really get to know my father.' Pherina cheerfully explains that in the Islands every household had a garden for food – banana, paw paw, taro and sweet potato. They didn't rely on buying things. 'In Auckland we had gardens too. When my grandmother came to New Zealand she planted vegies. They just can't help themselves!'

Pherina came to Australia with her partner and child in 1987. They came for a three week holiday, were offered jobs and have been here ever since. Now nearly her whole family is in Australia too, all her sisters and brothers. 'I've got three children, twenty-two and a ten-year-old and an eight-year-old.' She pauses and smiles with trepidation and more than a little glee. 'I have just found out I'm six months pregnant, so unexpected, I'm still trying to get over it!'

Pherina starts to talk about dancing and what it means to her. She explains seriously that in the Cook Islands, dancing and culture are like having breakfast, lunch and dinner. She didn't really like dancing until she went to New Zealand and her mother told her she had to learn. 'Then when I left school I met my partner, he was into dancing, culture, culture, culture. I suppose I was stuck with that. Everywhere we went it was dancing. I started dancing myself and just kept dancing. Since 1996 I have been teaching dancing to all kids, different ages.' Pherina formed her own dance group and they now perform all over Australia at festivals and similar events. 'So mostly the dance group now are family, and the drummers are myself, my partner, my brother-in-law and my sons. The dancers are all my sisters' and brothers' children. But I do teach Australians. They ring me for classes so I try to fit them in and I do teach Turkish and Aboriginal children. We've got the real hula skirts from the Cook Islands and the group are performing every weekend from now on. We are very busy, every festival. It's good for us because it's good for the kids. When we get the money we take out the expenses and then we share it between everybody and the kids get so happy because they've got pocket money and can pay for trips and excursions, camps. And we love doing it anyway. Sharing the culture.'

Pherina was instrumental in forming the Moonah. This is an organisation that helps with all sorts of problems and projects on the estate. It started with a group formed with the help of workers from the Coburg Health Centre, to deal with the problems on the estate. 'Everything started getting better because they would complain to me and I would say come into the group. Through that we started talking about having our own garden, that it would be nice. We looked for a spot and this is the spot we chose. It's made a big difference too, all the ladies around here used to stay indoors and now they come out and you get to talk to them. The garden has brought people together and got them talking to each other. They sit around here and talk about things and then you get to know them.' Pherina says that she knows everyone in the garden spreading her arms to encompass all the plots, Turkish, Australian, Somalian, Ethiopian, Islanders. 'A lot find it very hard to speak English but we do the hand language. We manage. We talk slowly and they will understand. They grow some very different plants; I'm always going "What's this? What do you use that for?" They do the same to us.' Pherina grows other vegetables but her main crop is taro.

The wide smile is never far from Pherina's face but she is serious when she describes how the kids on the estate were very bad, fighting and swearing. 'We needed something for the kids. Mostly they just wanted something to do.' So Pherina organised volleyball games with a string and an old ball. 'Some of them didn't know how to play, but we taught them, and every day we'd have games and the adults got into it too.' Pherina contacted the council to see if there was some way to get a proper net and ball. A week later she was told that they couldn't get the net and ball but they had managed to get $20 000 a year for three years. The broad grin spreads across her face again. 'I said, we only wanted a ball and a net! That's all we wanted, I didn't know that the ball and the net cost so much money.' They had managed to get a Vic Health grant. 'So all the ladies from around came to the meeting and that is how we formed Moonah and things just got better and better and the kids are really good and things started changing here. Our kids are so good it makes me feel good. Every school holidays we have family sports days that include sack races, water races, three legged races all that day.'

China

The Chinese people are very successful gardeners, getting maximum yields out of their plots all year round. They are mostly meticulously ordered and full of plants like *xian cai* or *yin choi* (amaranth), chillies, all the different Chinese cabbages, *gai cai* (mustard greens), *jiu cai* (garlic chives), *gou qi* or *kou kay* (Chinese boxthorn), *tong ho* (garland chrysanthemum), garlic, shallots, Chinese celery, perilla and spring onions.

Ai Mei Sun (Amy) and Qi Chi Zhao (Chitzu)

Ai Mei Sun (Amy) and Qi Chi Zhao (Chitzu)

Amy was born in Shanghai, China, where she lived with her parents and four siblings in a terrace house. They had a small open area where her mother grew flowers, mainly in pots. Her mother and father both worked in offices but she studied hard, went to university and graduated as a doctor. Amy was a paediatrician in a big hospital attached to a university. She is now retired.

Chitzu was born in the city of Suzhou, in South-East China near Shanghai. He shared his home with his mother, father, grandmother and six brothers and sisters. He says, 'I used to live in a very traditional Chinese house that included an old fashioned garden. My city is a famous tourist town in Jiangsu Province. There are many traditional houses and it is very, very beautiful. When I was young I remember that we had flowers and trees and herbs in the garden. It was very big.' Chitzu completed his primary and secondary schooling and then went to university in Hangzhou, the capital city of Zhejiang Province where he graduated in chemical engineering. He has worked in many different parts of China.

Amy and Chitzu married in about 1966 and have one son. After retiring, they came to Australia in January 1997 to be with their son, who had studied at RMIT and is working as a manager. They have only had a garden for a very short time and this is the first time they have tried to grow vegetables. This gentle, smiling couple radiate pleasure as they show us their garden. As Chitzu humbly says, 'We just try to watch how other people do it and if we fail then we will try again. I would love to swap plants but because of the language problems it is hard. They are interested in my vegetables but I can't tell them about them and I am interested in theirs but I don't know how to grow or use them.' Even so they have made friends with other gardeners and come to the garden twice a day, at seven in the morning and after seven at night. They also join in the activities like barbecues and go on trips to visit other people's gardens.

Despite their inexperience, their passion for their garden shines in their faces. It is a multicultural cornucopia of produce. As well as all the traditional Chinese plants they also grow Italian lettuce, tomatoes (red and yellow), purple king beans, *bian dou* (hyacinth beans), *dao dou* (soy beans), *dong gua* (winter melon), Lebanese cucumbers and eggplants, all squeezed into their tiny plot. They harvested over 100 cucumbers last year and say that although the land size is very small they are pleased with what they have been able to grow. Next year, however, they are determined to make their garden even better. Looking at its overflowing abundance it's hard to imagine how this could be done.

Mrs N. F. Poon

Mrs N. F. Poon

Mrs Poon was born in China in Hai Ping county, Guang Dong province. She grew up in a village where her father was a tailor and her mother looked after the house and grew the vegetables for the family. When she was thirteen her father passed away and at fourteen her mother died. Her brothers and sisters went to live with an aunt, but Mrs Poon, because she was the eldest, stayed in the house to look after it. She lived there by herself until she met her husband and married. A month later her husband went back to his pharmacy job in Hong Kong and Mrs Poon moved in with her parents-in-law and ran their farm. Quietly she explains, 'When we married I didn't go because at that time no women went to Hong Kong. In my village all the women stayed behind. The parents-in-law did not allow you to go overseas. We had to look after the house and do the farming. We had to look after the elderly people. We were not allowed to leave. Everybody was just like that. Whenever he could, my husband would return home and visit me.' Her gentle patience is obvious as she goes on to explain that the next phase of her life involved even more waiting.

Eventually, Mrs Poon and their two sons

moved to Hong Kong and then Mr Poon and the oldest son migrated to Australia. Mrs Poon and their younger son waited for a long time in Hong Kong before they were able to follow. Mr and Mrs Poon have been living in the flats since 1991 and now have six grandchildren. This diminutive grandmother who is in her eighties proudly tells us, 'All six have gone to university and are now working. One engineer, one architect, one secretary, one chemist, they are all very good!'

Mrs Poon has had a garden for more than ten years and says she loves growing the vegetables and visits twice a day. She grows many of the plants that she grew in China, and uses them in all her cooking. As well as the more common traditional plants she also grows things like *chi gu* (arrowhead), *gou qi* (Chinese boxthorn), nightshade and sweet potato leaves. Before planting, Mrs Poon digs cow manure into the soil and when the seedlings are starting to grow she adds a little blood and bone and then later adds some more blood and bone, and then as she puts it, 'That's it!' It obviously works because only the week before we spoke to her, she had made a meal for twenty, to celebrate her husband's birthday, and most of the vegetables were harvested from the garden. When asked what she cooked she replied with characteristic simplicity, 'I didn't make anything special, I just used all these vegetables to make ordinary dishes.'

Mrs Poon does not speak English and sadly says that if you cannot speak English it can be very frustrating. She seldom goes out now. This means that her garden is especially precious because it is one of the few places she can go to independently. Although she obviously misses much about her home and homeland, she says they did not have a doctor in their village, so people died and it was scary. 'When you are sick here, you can have easy access to doctors. I am very happy in Melbourne, my sons have their own houses and my grandchildren have graduated from the best university here.' Her eyes sparkle and there is a glimpse of a mischievous smile as this tiny, slender woman tells us, 'My grandsons are very tall, 6ft 3in. I'm very happy.'

Niu Jia Qi and Qian-xiu Chen

Niu Jia Qi

Niu Jia was born in 1919 in Hangzhou, Zhejiang Province in South West China. He says that Hangzhou is a very famous, beautiful place. Niu Jia's father was a mining engineer who worked mainly in coalmines. His mother died when he was only seven and his father remarried. Niu Jia went to school and university and graduated with a Bachelor of Medicine. He worked in medical microbiology and was a Professor of Medical Microbiology and Immunology. Niu Jia says that when he was young his family was very well off and he remembers a garden full of flowers: beautiful roses, hydrangeas, peaches, pears, cumquats and plums, all grown for their flowers. His father was the expert gardener. During the war the whole family moved to western China to escape the Japanese and the living conditions were not so good.

Later he married and has a son and two daughters. Niu Jia and his wife were visiting a married daughter in Australia when the Tianamin Square massacre happened and some of his friends advised them not to return to China. Eventually their visitors' visas were converted to permanent residency. Later Niu Jia's wife was badly injured in a car accident, so Niu Jia sponsored their son and his wife to come to Australia to care for them both. Niu Jia's wife died two years later and he has since remarried.

Niu Jia says he and his second wife Qianxiu Chen have had a garden for many years. Roguishly he tells us that his wife is younger so she does most of the digging. He adds, 'It is very good to have a garden for the exercise, I am very happy with it. I have not made many friends in the garden because they speak Cantonese and I speak Mandarin. If I talk to them they don't understand what I say. My wife can communicate with them, she speaks both Cantonese and Mandarin.' They grow most of the common Chinese vegetables as well as sweet potato leaves and several different beans, gourds and melons.

Niu Jia says that he eats more vegetables than meat and that he is fit and healthy for his age. He is aiming to live to be 100 and looks as if he'll make it. Every morning he walks in Royal Park which he says is a very, very beautiful place. He believes that there are five things elderly people need, 'They should have good accommodation or living space, good medical care, something to do, they should be useful and they should be happy.' He thinks that Australia does a pretty good job of providing these things. At present his only regrets are that he can't have more plots to grow more vegetables and he also very much wants to grow flowers, especially roses and peonies. He adds wistfully, 'It would be very beautiful to have flowers not only vegetables. We could plant a line of climbing roses and then it would look nicer.'

Shu Xian Li and Guo Guang Mei

Guo Guang was born in 1936 in Guang Dong province in South-East China. His father was a herbalist and his mother looked after the house and the five children. Guo Guang went to primary and secondary school and then moved by himself to

Shu Xian Li and Guo Guang Mei

Nanjing where he studied to be an electrician. 'It was not hard to move, at that time, I was young I liked going my own way, living my own life.' While studying he met his wife and has now been married for more than forty years.

Shu Xian was born in Nanjing where her family has lived for three or four generations. Her father was a western medical doctor and her eight brothers and sisters all became doctors too. Shu Xian trained with her husband but became an electronics expert, working in long distance communications. All of her siblings are still in China. Shu Xian says, 'I started by loving everything natural, everything in nature, when I was a student. Every time when the school went on excursions I saw and loved plants, flowers, clouds in the sky, everything in nature.'

They have two children; their daughter is in Australia, and their son is still in Nanjing. Guo Guang and Shu Xian have been in Australia for more than seven years and have returned to China to see their son twice. When they first came, they lived with their daughter but later moved into the flats, although Shu Xian goes back to stay with her daughter and two grandchildren from time to time because she misses them so much. Shu Xian seems sad as she tells us, 'When I lived in my daughter's house they had a very big garden. I loved it. I grew a lot of flowers there, many, many flowers. But after I moved here my daughter and her husband were too busy to look after it.'

They have had a plot in the community gardens for about three years, and Guo Guang says, 'The garden is the only thing that is important to her, I am not really interested but I go occasionally to look after it for her.' Shu Xian carefully explains that the people in the community garden are from everywhere around the world, but because she does not speak the same language she cannot communicate with them – they just say hello and smile and look at each other's plants. She adds that they often share plants and seeds with the other gardeners. But gardening is not always friendly. Regretfully Shu Xian explains that she was growing some roses, which she loves, but someone poured petrol on them and killed them and the garden. She was heart-broken and decided to abandon her garden. But the garden worker, who looked after the garden, was very kind and changed all the earth for her. 'Even though it was raining they still kept working.' Shu Xian really appreciated their hard work and kindness, and decided to continue working in the garden. She grows unusual varieties of capsicum and chillies as well as the usual Chinese vegetables, and leeks, garlic, daikon, snake beans and even small plants of sugar cane. Shu Xian beautifully sums up her passion for gardening when she says, 'This garden is my lover.'

the people

Middle East

The Middle Eastern people of the community gardens are from countries like Iran, Iraq, Afghanistan and Turkey. They have come to Australia for a variety of reasons although the theme of war, upheaval and loss is common. They grow many of the plants that would be grown in their homelands including coriander, tomatoes, capsicums, chillies, onions, garlic, cucumbers, beans, potatoes, silver beet, parsley, chives, mint, basil and oregano.

Wajia Noori, Aghdas Nasr and Basira Wasil

Wajia Noori, Aghdas Nasr and Basira Wasil

Aghdas Nasr

Aghdas was born in Esfahān, Iran. She explains that this city used to be the capital of ancient Persia so that it has many historic and very beautiful buildings. Both her parents were farmers and keen gardeners. 'They lived in the country with a big yard and big garden. When I was growing up my parents grew beans and chickpeas to sell and then when I got older they changed over and mainly grew fruit trees like cherries and apples. They also grew all kinds of herbs like parsley and basil for the family. We didn't grow the herbs for medicine, they were mainly for eating. Iranians like to have the herbs on the table and eat them fresh.' After she married, Aghdas' home was a modern building with a communal pool and sauna. She also had a little bit of garden, surrounded by glass, where she grew flowers.

Aghdas came to Australia because her son was living here and now she has that son and six daughters all living in Melbourne. They are all working or studying and she says they don't have time to garden but she loves her garden because it enables her to use fresh herbs to make her children's favourite dishes. 'My children love these dishes so my garden grows these particular herbs to make these dishes.' Her children are obviously her life and her all embracing warmth also extends to her friends. 'I love working in the garden, I go to the garden every morning to check it and it is a good meeting place. The mosaic tables and chairs, that is our meeting place in the summer. We have a chat and a cup of tea together, and somebody might make a cake, we have a good time.'

Wajia Noori and Basira Wasil

Wajia was born in the suburb of Daroulaman in Kabul, Afghanistan. 'Before the war we had a very big house and a big garden and we had a lot of flowers and herbs in the garden. Both my parents were very keen gardeners. My father worked in the house so they both loved the flowers and planted the flowers. I got married during the war and went to live with my husband. After the war everything was ruined, my house was ruined. All the houses got ruined and all the windows were broken, houses were flattened, gardens were all dug up. We came to Australia because there was nowhere to live and Afghanistan was totally ruined after twenty-five years of war. I was a teacher. We lost everything; that is why we left. If we still had our houses and the country wasn't ruined we wouldn't have left.' Wajia's sadness is almost palpable but she brightens a little as she goes on to tell us that she and her husband have one daughter, the light of their lives, and that she is in Year 8 at high school. 'Back home we had a beautiful garden, the garden here keeps home close to me. I think of home, it makes me happy. I like to grow herbs and vegetables. I come to tend my garden every day. My daughter helps in the garden, she loves it.'

Basira was born in Afghanistan, also in Daroulaman and says she knew Wajia but they didn't become friends until they came to Australia. 'My parents had a big house and the house was very tall and they had a big garden and they had all kinds of fruits like apricots and nectarines, peaches, cherries. We didn't sell much but gave a

AFGHANI RECIPE FROM WAJIA

KABAB DASHI

2 cups water
1 onion, chopped
1 clove garlic, finely chopped
1 kg lamb, trimmed of any fat and diced
½ cup olive oil
1 kg onions, sliced
¼ teaspoon salt
1 tablespoon whole coriander seed
freshly ground black pepper
fresh mint leaves
Lebanese flat bread

Bring water to the boil in a saucepan. Add the chopped onion, garlic and meat and lower heat to simmer gently. Cook, uncovered, until water has evaporated and then gently continue to 'fry' the meat, stirring, for a few more minutes. In a large frying pan, add the oil and gently fry the onion slices until tender. Drain the oil. Add the cooked meat to the frying pan with the onions, add salt and cook, stirring, for approximately 1 minute. Place the meat and onion mix onto a serving platter. Grind the coriander seed and sprinkle over the meat. Add a little bit of black pepper and decorate with mint leaves. Eat it by spooning it inside Lebanese flat bread. **Serves 4–6.**

lot to friends and especially to poor people who didn't have anything. They would get free fruit from the trees. We had all kinds of vegetables, like tomatoes, eggplant, potatoes, onions, whatever you liked we had them.' This strong, slender woman who has endured so much has now been in Australia for more than two years and quietly explains how important the garden is to her. 'I come down for the good fresh air and the green. It brings back the good memories from home. I come down to the garden most days.' Basira has a son in Year 11 at high school. 'When he is free, not studying, he comes and helps.'

The Afghani women did not talk much about the war in Afghanistan or their reasons for coming to Australia or the traumas they experienced in getting here. Wajia and Basira told us that they came on the same boat to Darwin and spent several months in the Port Hedland detention centre. They very much want to look towards a settled and secure future for themselves and their families and wanted us to know that they were very worried about being on temporary visas. 'We Afghanis, if you look, live very modestly, we don't go out and spend money, we live a very simple life, but there is no life in Afghanistan, the Taliban is still there, they haven't got rid of them. We love the Australian people, they are very nice and kind but where are we going to go? We have nothing left.'

Sabri and Hatice Kiziltan

Sabri was born in a small town called Zara in central Turkey but spent most of his childhood in Susehri. Nostalgically Sabri explains that Susehri is famous for its gardens and huge orchards of fruit trees, adding that it has very fertile soil. 'Everyone has their own garden and in summer they live in their gardens and in winter months they move back to the town. Some of the gardens are situated right in the town but others were 45 minutes' walk away. In the town we had a proper house, but we also had a summerhouse, like a two-bedroom shack, in the gardens.' Sabri has five siblings, his father was a public servant and his mother looked after the house and the garden. They grew many different fruit trees and stored the hard fruit, made jams from the soft fruit and extracted juice, called *pekmez*, from the grapes. Sabri went to school until he was seventeen when he left and went to Ankara. Two years later he did two years of compulsory national service and then made a living driving taxis. Later he upgraded his licence to drive trucks and buses. Sabri's weathered face splits into a lively grin as he explains

Sabri and Hatice Kiziltan

that he came to Australia in 1973 because it was an adventure, he remembers reading about Australia in geography and he was very curious to see it.

Hatice was born in Ankara, Turkey, in 1948. She came from a big family with four siblings, her parents and her paternal grandmother. They all lived in a big house with a garden large enough to grow their own vegetables. Hatice's father was a manager with the State railways and her mother looked after the house and garden with the help of Hatice's grandmother. They also had chickens. Hatice left school when she was about thirteen because of serious health problems. She spent a lot of time in hospital. She gradually recovered, trained to be a hairdresser, worked for two years and then married Sabri when she was only seventeen. Both Sabri and Hatice's siblings are still in Turkey.

'When we came to Australia it was a new place, we were excited, we thought it would be good for the children, for their future. The youngest was two and a half years old, the oldest about five and a half. They all started school here, picked up English and settled in quickly.' Hatice's gentle, calm face softens as she contemplates her children. 'We have four children. The daughter is married now with one grandchild. The boys are single but they are all adults. They all live near and they drop in three or four times a week.' Sabri

and Hatice are happy in Australia but they still miss Turkey. 'It is not just that it is my home, my country, but it is really a beautiful country, the seasons go by the calendar, you have three months of everything, four seasons,' Hatice wistfully explains.

Sabri and Hatice have lived in the area for a long time. Sabri helped to construct the paths at the Collingwood Children's Farm and had a garden plot there for many years. Sabri gazes fondly at the garden plot that he's now had for more than two years. It is like another room in his home, with pictures and statues, somewhere of great importance. He wryly smiles and explains: 'I learnt a lot from my mother and I see this garden as one of my children, I spend most of my days here.' Hatice nods and quietly defines his devotion. 'The garden is his life, he gets rid of his stress in the garden, he speaks to the plants and vegetables, he shares things with them.' Sabri goes on to say that they have made many friends in the garden. 'We enjoy our garden because the produce is fresh, it is organic, it is all natural, it tastes much better.'

Zeyneb Turker

Zeyneb Turker

Zeyneb was born on the Mediterranean Sea in Korzan, Adana, Turkey. She smiles as she reminisces about the beauty of Adana. 'We had a beautiful life, it was very green, a lot of fields. My parents were farmers. They grew cotton and wheat and fruit, mainly lemons and oranges. I helped them a little bit on the farm, although I had seven brothers, and two sisters who were much older. I was the only girl at home so I had to stay home and look after their clothes; ironing, washing, cooking, while they were all out working.' Zeyneb went to school for about five years and then at seventeen married a man from the same village, and soon after migrated to Australia.

'When we came we didn't know anyone in Australia. My husband wanted to come. My family didn't want me to go. My husband promised to send me home to Turkey every four to five years.' She shrugs her acceptance when she adds that they have been in Australia for thirty-five years, and she has been back to Turkey five times. Zeyneb worked for Holeproof and then Bradmill and ended up as a supervisor. Her husband worked for GMH and Uncle Toby's. 'My daughter and son both finished university doing computer programming and my son has done a second Masters. Both work and have good jobs.' Her pride in her children is pronounced. With a mischievous grin Zeyneb tells us that her one luxury is to go to bingo three times a week. 'I don't win very often!'

Zeyneb contemplates her garden and says, 'Having a garden here is very special to me. When I have too many problems I sit down in the garden and I just look and have a smoke and coffee and I'm relaxed and I forget about all my problems. I have many friends in the garden, Turkish, Vietnamese, Chinese and Australian. It is very friendly. We always give each other seed. We love it here, sometimes in the summer time we are here until 1 am.' Zeyneb grows *tere* (cress), *kara lahana* (kale) and nettles as well as all the more common vegetables and herbs. 'I love gardening' she exclaims, 'My garden is always tidy, I never make a mess.' While she is talking, Zeyneb is rapidly picking produce from her garden, putting it into Turkish bread and handing it out for others to eat – parsley, lettuce, rocket, basil, spring onions and mint. 'Everything,' says Zeyneb. 'This is very healthy, you can't buy it in the shop. It's delicious.'

East Timor

The people in these interviews mostly left East Timor at the time of, or soon after, the Indonesian annexation of their country in 1976, either coming straight to Australia or going first to Portugal and then to Australia. The climate in East Timor is mainly tropical and the plants grown there reflect this. In temperate Melbourne, the East Timorese achieve remarkable success by still growing the plants of their homeland, things like *fehuk-midar tahan* (sweet potato leaves), *forei talin* (snake beans), Chinese broccoli and cabbages, *mustarda* (mustard greens), taro, nightshade and chillies.

Ana Martins

Ana was born in the village of Letefoho, East Timor. 'In my family we had three girls and five boys. Only the two youngest ones went to school. The oldest ones had to work hard to find the money to pay for the two youngest ones, for uniforms and books and other necessities.' Ana radiates warmth and acceptance as she explores the memories of her early life. Her family were farmers. 'My family owned all this land, my uncle, auntie, relatives, we all just shared the land together and worked together.' They grew coffee and tea to sell and vegetables like corn, taro, cassava, sweet potato, mustard, choko and eggplants for the family. Tomatoes grew wild. They also had a fish farm and cows, sheep, a few chickens, a horse and pigs. 'It was very hard work if you had a farm, you had to carry water and when you come home you had to have some firewood. If you have an elderly person at home you have to nurse them and you have to boil water to have a bath. Saturday was laundry time so we went to the creek to do our washing. We would have a shower there or wash our hair. And then on Sunday we went to Mass. We walked. It took about an

Ana Martins

hour to get there and if you are with kids that is about two hours and some were too little to walk so we had to carry them.' Ana lived in the village until she was in her twenties when she moved to Dili.

Later Ana came to Australia and in 1976 met and married an Australian man. They moved to Shepparton where they bought a ten acre market garden and grew vegetables that they sold at the Footscray market. 'We had the farm for five years. Then I had my younger child and we were unable to keep up the mortgage any more so the bank took over. I left my husband because he was very lazy and I moved back to Melbourne,' Ana explains with her natural openness.

She has five children altogether, all now in Australia although one has gone back to East Timor to work for the UN. Her beautiful smile warms those around her as she tells us that she is happy in Australia and her garden is an important part of this. 'If I don't have anything to do I can talk to my vegetables, it's a pleasure to have a little garden and do something with it. In the garden everyone is my friend. We share our plants. I look after the grandchildren. I come to the garden every second day. I can look at it from my window. Sometimes if I don't come, Joana will help me with the watering.'

Ana grows her traditional plants as well as onions, corn, garlic, lettuce, carrots, mustard, broad beans, snow peas and even wheat. Neither space nor produce goes to waste. The snow peas grow up bamboo tripods, all parts of the taro are eaten (leaf, stem and root) and the stems are used medicinally. Ana also grows nightshade. 'We eat it, it is good for high blood pressure and for diabetes.'

Edite H. Ku

Edite H. Ku

Edite was born in Dili, East Timor, one of seven children. They lived in a house with a garden where they grew sweet potatoes, Chinese vegies, snake beans and tomatoes. 'My mother was the gardener but when we grew up we helped mother with the planting as well. That is how I learned to garden. The soil was very good. We used the skin from the winter melon and some other melons as natural fertilisers. They make the soil rich. We didn't chop the skin, we just put it on the surface of the soil.' They also had chickens, pigs and ducks.

In her unassuming way Edite explains that she only finished grade three at school. 'Because of the hardship in the family, I just helped my mother with the housework and looking after my younger sisters and brothers.' She came to Australia in 1981 with her whole family – parents, siblings, husband and son – except for three older siblings who stayed in East Timor. She has only had a garden for a few years and her pleasure in her garden is easy to see. 'I come to the garden to relax myself and spend some time here. I have made many, many friends in the garden. Every day I take my grandchild to the school and then come to the garden. And in the afternoon I come as well. I love coming here. I share plants and seeds with other gardeners and they share back with me. We help each other.' Edite mostly grows plants from her homeland and her plot teems with evidence of her skill. 'I save the seeds from all my plants. I don't buy seeds.'

Joana Barreto

Joana Barreto

Joana was born in Ermera, East Timor. 'It was quite a big place with a lot of coffee plantations. We had a coffee plantation; it belonged to mum and dad. My father was like a king of that village. The coffee plantation was huge. We had a lot of help, the children and the grandchildren.' Joana was the youngest of five children. She waves her work worn hands, that are never still when she is in the garden, as she explains, 'I never went to school because we had to look after the plantation and the garden and the rice field. So that was my life. When we needed to do the rice field then we got the cattle to do the job. We also had chickens and pigs. All of them just living wild and when we wanted them we would catch them. My grandfather, if we didn't work, he would beat us. We had to help with many things, the house duties, the cleaning and washing, take care of my uncle's children and then I had to work in the rice field and the plantation. When mum and dad passed away I lived with my grandparents, but because my grandfather was so very strict I ran away to a nunnery in Dili. I lived there for about ten years cooking for the girls who stayed in the nunnery and the teachers, hundreds of them. That was my duty.'

In 1971 Joana went to Portugal and then in 1985 came to Australia. She did not originally intend to stay in Australia but with her impish smile she explains, 'I have my roots here, my own place. I like my single life, because I never married and I like to have a bit of wandering and I like this life. I went back to Portugal twice and in 1991 I went to visit East Timor. After so many years things change.'

Joana has had a garden for seventeen years. 'In Timor I already had the habit of growing and working in the garden. So when I came here this is my life, I love so much to do this. There are so many different people that actually have a garden. They are friends but each friend, I don't really know their heart because I don't want to get too involved as this can create problems and I don't like this. I come to the garden every day at 5 o'clock, 6 o'clock, but sometimes I sleep in and I come down at 7 o'clock.'

Joana's garden is full to overflowing with traditional vegetables. She also loves to care for the worm farm and uses both the liquid and the castings in her garden. She is involved in every activity in the gardens and being the social and gregarious person she is, loves to go on the organised excursions and be there for the celebrations and barbecues. She does not think that she will go back to Portugal or Timor again as it would cost too much money and although she does have some relatives left in Timor, she poignantly adds, 'I don't have any more siblings, or father or mother or grandfather. I am the only one left.'

Tju Ing Chung

Tju Ing is of Chinese descent and was born in East Timor, in Liquica about one hour from Dili. She is one of ten children. 'My father and the children looked after the garden together. My father loved to grow fruit and my brother and I loved to grow flowers. My sister loved to grow vegetables – sweet potatoes, snake beans, pumpkin, winter melon, garlic chives and spring onions.' Tju Ing's father taught Chinese at a primary school some distance from where they lived, so he stayed with a nearby friend and returned home during the holidays; her mother was a housewife. Tju Ing went to high school for a few years and then worked helping her mother and sister to sell prepared meals to take away. 'My mother cooked very simple meals and we just sold them to the local people from our house. My mother also grew the fruit that we sold, made the bread and roasted the coffee. Every Thursday was market day and we were very busy preparing bread and coffee. This way we made a little money for the future.'

When she was seventeen, the whole family moved to Dili to find better jobs and there Tju Ing worked as a shop assistant and in her spare time made clothes to sell. Like many other Timorese, Tju Ing was accepted into Portugal as a refugee and stayed there for three years before coming to Australia in 1981, where she quickly found a sewing job in a factory. 'I met my husband in Australia and I got married here. My mother and the rest of my family are here too. I have been living in these flats for fourteen years and the people here introduced me to my husband. He had come from East Timor, just for a visit.'

Tju Ing Chung

Tju Ing and her husband have two children, a girl and a boy. Quietly she explains that she loves to grow vegetables to eat and mostly she grows those things she grew at home in Timor. 'Sometimes when I am doing my planting here I really miss those days when I was growing my own vegetables and flowers. I still remember the beautiful flowers that I grew.'

the people

Eastern Europe

The gardeners from Eastern Europe have come to Australia either because of political upheaval in their home countries or to follow children who left for these reasons. Their gardens and gardening reflect the temperate climate of their homelands, especially the cold winters, with vegetables like lettuces, black radishes, onions, tomatoes, beetroots and potatoes as well as herbs such as marigolds, sorrel, dill, plantain, nettles and parsley.

Ida Paskovatia

Ida was born in Ukraine, in Kamenets-Podolskiy. Her parents did not have a garden. 'It was all concrete and there was no place or space for gardening.' During the war, when she was about seventeen, Ida and her family moved to Russia and here she started gardening. Ida says that she was assigned to a special team of people who were called 'The Vegetable Brigade'. She learnt many things. 'You know that if you love soil, the soil gives her response, she gives some things back. It was really very interesting and no matter where I lived or where I live now, I can't go on without a small piece of land.' Ida has no brothers or sisters as they were all killed during the war, but her father, who was disabled during the civil war, survived the Second World War and went on to live for 102 years. 'I remember, my Dad got up very, very early in the morning and he used to bring the strawberries from the forest and all the children had them in summer. He was a very, very good father, the best father in the whole world. He always had a lot of friends. He was a person with a gold heart.'

Ida Paskovatia

After the war Ida moved back to Kamenets-Podolskiy, married and stayed there until she came to Australia. This vivacious, charming, elderly woman is over eighty and has two children, a boy and a girl. Her daughter lives in Melbourne. 'I didn't see my daughter for twelve years and now I don't see my son. But we can do nothing. I don't love those two oceans that separate us.' Ida's son lives in America.

All Ida's seedlings are home grown, as she believes that bought seedlings are no good. She improves her soil with compost made from organic vegetables, and fertilises with manure obtained from healthy animals. Her other gardening secret is the use of water, stored in bottles left in the sun. 'Melbourne water is very good but it's not enough. I use the solar energy to make the water strong. It is like charging the water with solar energy. It is special water.'

Ida proudly shows us her beautiful bush strawberries, the same that grew wild in the forests near her home. She says that they are juicy and taste exactly like in her native town. She also grows several different tomatoes and a variety of herbs including a plant she calls milkweed (greater celandine).

The abundant enthusiasm for life and her garden are obvious but her family are equally important. Ida sees her daughter often. 'She has a very good heart and I'm telling her that she inherited that from my Dad. She is ready to help anyone. My daughter cooks for me and brings ready prepared meals.' Ida suffers from panic attacks. 'Sometimes I have attacks and I can't do anything at all. I can't go outside. Sometimes I don't want to communicate with people and I don't want to go out. But when I come here (to the garden) and see all this, this is my world, this is my peace.'

Mendel Vorobeychik

Mendel was born in 1922 in Vitebsk, in what was then Belorussia (now the Republic of Belarus). His father worked in a shoe factory and his mother was a process worker. 'My mother was a very enthusiastic supporter of socialism and the new society. When the Government said we need some help she just took off her ear-rings and ring, that was all the gold she had, and she gave it to them absolutely.' Mendel says that his family was very poor and that he can remember in 1937, when everyone was starving, that his father brought home some bread, just a little loaf, it was cut into many, many pieces to make it last. 'I just remember how special that bread was, how difficult it was to get, we were just sitting and very slowly savouring it.'

Partly because of poverty but also because of a disability, Mendel only completed about six years of schooling, but ever since he was little he can remember loving to draw; he drew pictures of the weapons of the time and huge portraits of Marx, Engels and Lenin. He still loves to draw and paint today. When he stopped school, Mendel started work in a needle factory where he

Mendel Vorobeychik

was given the most difficult task of putting the eyes in the tiniest needles. In the evenings he went to compulsory night school. Later he trained as a watchmaker, working with some of the smallest watches and becoming a specialist in this trade.

In 1941, during the war, Mendel and his mother and sister were evacuated to a small rural village. His father was sent to fight (and later die) and six months later Mendel was also drafted. He was sent first to the Chinese border and then fought and was wounded in Stalingrad. His mother and sister were moved to the Ural Mountains and Mendel joined them, working as a guard. Then he was sent as a junior lieutenant to support the storming of Koeningsberg in Germany. Here he was wounded again and by the time he left hospital the war had ended.

Mendel settled in Bobrujsk, in Belarus, where his mother and sister joined him and he later married. His sister still lives there. He went back to working as a watchmaker and continued this work until he migrated to Australia with his two daughters in the 70s.

Mendel grows his own vegetables and herbs, but he also spends a lot of time helping his friends and neighbours. Ida explains, 'All of the people who live here, anything that they need fixed they always come to him, watches and clocks and little things. He knows how to do all this. He is very important for our garden too, he is almost like a magic wand, every time we want something he is ready to do it, he is very, very, careful with very good hands. When we think of something his hands always come to the rescue.'

He smiles his gentle smile and mildly adds, 'I feel very useful and very comfortable helping so much in the garden.'

Adelina Vasileva

Adelina was born in Kiev, the capital of Ukraine. Both her parents were engineers and after finishing technical school with straight A's she also became an engineer. 'I worked for a construction company that was doing construction and renovation to all the cultural places, like the various clubs and cinemas. We were mainly working with rebuilding things. Thirty-six years I worked in the same place, in the same profession.' Adelina's husband was a fitter and turner, 'He was a worker, a very intelligent person but he preferred working with his hands.'

They came to Australia in 1994, although it took them a long time to make the decision. Quietly, Adelina articulates some of the pain of so many immigrants. 'I understand that Australia is a much better country but my heart is still with my motherland and no matter how bad it is there, it is still my motherland and I don't hide that, but here I have confidence in tomorrow, because Australia does not let aged people vanish or be in poverty.'

Adelina's parents did not have a garden in Kiev. 'Before this garden I have never

Adelina Vasileva

had a garden and have never touched land in my life, but now I am so enamoured with my garden that I cannot go to sleep without coming and visiting it.' Adelina has discovered that she has a green thumb, but her garden also affects her on a deeper level and she pauses to gravely express what she wants to say: 'This garden for me is something for the soul, something very spiritual. I believe that I really draw some energy from it.' Adelina has two adult children and her daughter has a garden at her home, but with a wry smile Adelina observes, 'Who works there? I work there! My grandchildren love to spend their time here, in my garden, with me. They like to dig and they like to pull out the parsley and put it in the soup and then they are so happy that they did some gardening.'

Adelina is a thoughtful person and another issue she ponders is the value of families. 'Educating and bringing your children up well is like putting money in the bank with high interest. The more effort you put into your children the more interest you get later on.' But her thoughts never stray far from her garden. 'Last year I had tomatoes and everyone was coming to see what tomatoes I had and how many and how beautiful they were. And my potato plants were also very beautiful.' As well as vegetables, Adelina grows herbs, like marigolds and parsley, for their culinary and medicinal uses. 'I have a sister and she lives in New York and she has a very similar garden to mine and sometimes we exchange notes on the kind of things that have grown in her garden and haven't grown in mine. When I have winter, she has summer so our seasons are mixed.'

Kapitolina Ruburovska

Kapitolina Ruburovska

Although Kapitolina's parents are Russian, she was born in China in a village called Mergen near the city of Kharbin. In 1955, when Kapitolina was seven years old, her mother took the family back to Russia, to Vladivostock. Her father remained in China but eventually migrated to Australia where he now lives.

Kapitolina says that her mother wanted to live with Russians again and they were promised a good life by the Soviets when they took them out of China. Shrugging philosophically she quietly explains that life was a struggle. 'My mother had three of us and she found it very difficult to take care of us. I had two brothers, they were wonderful brothers. From a young age we were always in the vegetable patch, without this vegetable garden, we wouldn't have survived. Mum was too busy because she worked but we always had our vegetables and we always made sure we did the growing. The soil was reasonable but we did a lot of fertilising and we always made quite a lot of compost and used that to make sure that the soil was good. The fish bone meal was wonderful for the garden too. We grew everything! Autumn was always the busiest time of the year because we were trying to preserve the vegetables for winter. We made preserves, everything you can think of was put into the jars.' Kapitolina became a kindergarten teacher, married and has a son still living in Russia. Her beloved brothers died young.

Kapitolina has only had her garden for

a short time but already she is growing her favourite herbs and vegetables. She uses her plants for cooking and medicine. 'I very much enjoy having my garden plot because I really love gardens.' Her only regret is that she does not have more space.

Oscar Jeney

Oscar Jeney

Oscar was born in Budapest, Hungary. There were three children, two boys and a girl. Oscar was the oldest and was only six or seven when the whole family migrated to Australia during the Hungarian revolution. 'My father was a fitter and turner, and my mother learnt the trade of pleating, in clothes like a skirt, it is very steamy work, her hands used to be quite rough. You had to have a start somewhere.' After renting for a while they saved up to buy a house. Even on vendor's terms, this seemed 'beyond imagination' to a young migrant family.

Oscar went to RMIT to study fashion design. 'I was really interested in this because it was creative. I was also a member of the Melbourne Artists' Society in the very early days. After RMIT I worked for a sports clothing manufacturer designing skirts and tracksuits and things like that.' Later Oscar worked for another company, then he married and had a family, two boys and a girl. Later again he ran his own very successful fashion business.

Oscar moved into the flats about six years ago and then three years ago started on the gardens. 'This community project was the garden, we established the garden, we got a lot of help from the local council. I'm quite happy that within the public housing estate we have something that is communal and keeps people together with a common interest. Like producing and being creative. The new tenants have really grabbed the idea of having their own vegetable plots.' Oscar confidently says he has learnt a lot of new skills since he started gardening. He sprouts his own seeds and gives lots away.

Oscar's all-embracing enthusiasm and knowledge of these gardens is evident as he tells of a person who had been cooped up in her flat for the past seven years. 'She came down one day and talked to me and said she would like a garden plot and since then she is so active that everyone knows her. It is therapeutic for her. The garden management, Cultivating Community has been very helpful giving us advice and more understanding of how to care for our gardens. We also got some free liquid sea-weed fertiliser, we used it and saw that the result was good so we now have quite a lot of knowledge under our belts for next year to be able to start up and have everything quite creative and happy.'

Oscar grows many different vegetables and has experimented with cuttings from tomatoes and chillies to produce new plants. He also has an interest in the medicinal uses of plants and in particular has been researching the uses of marigolds. He now has five grandchildren. 'My family is so happy that I have the garden because all of my grandkids, they all love my cherry tomatoes, they are mad about them.'

Lioudmila Karmacheva

Lioudmila Karmacheva

Lioudmila was born in the old USSR in the capital city of Turkmenistan, now called Ashgabat. Her father was a transport communications engineer and her mother a secretary at a technical college. Their lives changed dramatically during the war when her father was killed and then again in 1948 when the city was all but destroyed by a huge earthquake. Lioudmila says that 100 000 people were killed, including her only brother who was ten; she was fifteen. The earthquake victims were evacuated to other cities and Lioudmila and her mother ended up in the Russian city of Saratov. They were very poor but she was able to go to university where she graduated as a chemist. She married – her husband was also a chemist – had two children and worked for the next three decades for the Cosmic Research Laboratories that were well known for their important and secret research.

After thirty years of work, the Government gave Lioudmila 600 square metres of land. It was virgin, unworked soil and was 50 kilometres away from where she lived and worked. Lioudmila would wake at six and take the train to her land, work on it for a short time and race back to work. After seven years it was a garden with more than twenty fruit trees, black currants, raspberries and all the vegetables. Smiling broadly Lioudmila explains that she fell in love with her garden and kept working there even under the most difficult conditions. The growing season was only five months, and although they could pump water from the Volga ten kilometres away, she remembers that for spring planting there was absolutely no water because the Volga was under ice. 'In March we were up to our chests in snow and we would shovel the snow into our water container and as this melted we would use it to water the spring planting. From February my home was full of little containers, rows and rows, where I would plant the seeds and grow the seedlings. Then we would plant them out. Other people also had plots of land nearby. They were enthusiastic too because without gardens it was very difficult to survive. But it was not just for money or for food, it was also to feel yourself part of humanity. Land is a gloriously magic thing, it gives us so much.'

Lioudmila came to Australia to join her children and grandchildren. She is still a dedicated gardener. 'I have had a garden for about three years. I enjoy the garden, it doesn't matter how much, how big, but I like plants. To work the land, I love the contact. I have friends in the garden.' She is a picture of good health and also very fit. Every morning, winter and summer, she catches the train to Brighton to swim. Lioudmila believes that this and the fresh vegetables and herbs, especially marigolds, black radishes and onions from her garden, keep her fit and healthy.

the plants

Aloe vera

Aloe vera

Aloe vera is a succulent perennial that can reach 70 cm but is usually smaller. It grows as a cluster of very fleshy thick leaves, with prickly margins and no stems; usually the leaves have white spots. The orange-yellow flowers grow in spikes.

Grow

Aloes like hot, dry conditions and very good drainage. If allowed to stay wet the plant will rot at the base and die. They will also be killed by a heavy frost. New plants can be grown by carefully removing and replanting the small suckers that grow around the base of an existing plant.

Garden talk

Aloe vera is used by almost all the cultures represented in the gardens. They use it for burns, bites, stings, rashes and other skin complaints. Just cut off a section of leaf, slice it lengthwise and rub the sap onto the skin. Ida maintains that she uses it for 'everything', while Julia massages the sap into her face and says that if it is taken internally, after being boiled in water, it is very good to cleanse the body. Vilma agrees and laughingly adds, 'It improves your skin so that you look lovely.' Tai uses the sap. 'You just put it on the area where it is itching, and for constipation, just cook it and drink the water.' Ruyet explains that if you don't like the taste you can add a little honey. Maria uses it mainly to treat wounds, especially those she gets while working in the garden.

Aloe vera

Amaranth (Chinese spinach)

Amaranth

Amaranthus sp.

Amaranthus species are grown throughout the world for both their seeds and leaves. Leaf amaranth comes in three different species: Chinese spinach also known as Asian red spinach (*A. tricolor*), the plant grown and most used in Asia; as well as purple amaranth (*A. lividis*) and green amaranth (*A. viridis*), both widely used in the Mediterranean and South America. Amaranth is an annual that grows to over 1 m with fleshy thick stems. Leaf shape is highly variable but usually oval, and the colour green or purple, or a combination of the two. The flowers are generally green or red and occur in terminal spikes.

Grow
Grow from seed sown into the garden in spring. Thin to about 15 cm between plants. Amaranth needs well-com-posted soil high in nutrients, but apart from this is not fussy. It also likes full, hot sun and plenty of water during dry periods. Begin to harvest the leaves as soon as plants are big enough. Once flowers appear the leaves are starting to get tough. Plants self-sow readily.

Garden talk
Amaranth leaves have a sweet but tangy flavour. As they are fairly high in both nitrates and oxalic acid don't eat them fresh too often, although young leaves can occasionally be added to salad. Mostly, the leaves are boiled and the water discarded before eating. Ruyet calls amaranth *rau den* and adds it to soup with prawn or pork. 'It will cool down the inside of the body.' Leaves are high in vitamin C, carotene, calcium, folic acid and protein and they contain twice as much iron as ordinary spinach. Mrs Poon says that she fries

the leaves in the same way as sweet potato leaves. Amy and Chitzu are not fussy about which amaranth they use, with all the colours growing in their garden. Niu Jia uses it in soup or just fries it, and adds that he loves this plant because it grows so fast. Julia says that they mainly use the green ama-ranth. 'The red one is more ashamed than the other one, that is why it went red', she adds laughing. Maria main-tains that amaranth, which she calls *vleeta*, is like spinach, but sweeter and softer. She uses it in salads, with filo pastry and with rice but always steams or blanches it first. Amaranth stems are also eaten, usually peeled first and then steamed.

GREEK RECIPE FROM DINA
Vleeta

salt
500g amaranth leaves, washed
olive oil
lemon juice or vinegar

Bring a large pot of water to the boil and add a good pinch of salt. Add amaranth leaves and boil until tender (about 5 min-utes). Drain well, season to taste with olive oil and lemon juice or vinegar, and serve. **Serves 2**.

Arrowhead
Sagittaria sagittifolia

Arrowhead

Arrowhead is a perennial plant that grows to about 70 cm from spherical, brownish-yellow corms. The leaves grow on long slender stems and are pale green and shaped like arrowheads. The three-petalled flowers are white with a yellow centre.

Grow
Arrowhead can be planted on the edge of a pond, or grown in a bath-tub or

similar container. It does best with 100–300 mm of water over the soil; the colder the climate the more shallow the water should be. Plant corms in spring by pushing them down into mud that has been enriched with cow manure. Choose a sunny position and space the corms about 30 cm apart. Horizontal rhizomes grow from the central corm and a new corm will grow at the end of each rhizome. Harvest corms in autumn.

Garden talk

Young shoots and leaves are eaten raw or cooked, but corms are always cooked.

They are peeled and sliced, then fried or added to stews. Mrs Poon says that these are similar to taro. They have a slightly sweet taste. 'You have to peel off the skin and mash it. Mix it with some Chinese sausages and some celery and then fry it together. It is crispy like water chestnuts.' Corms are also boiled, roasted and baked, or chopped and fried to make chips. Mrs Poon grows new plants by replanting the corms, or by just pushing some of the leaves, with stems, into the soil.

Basil

Ocimum spp.

Sweet basil

Many different basils are grown and used in the gardens. Gardeners from Asian backgrounds usually grow Thai basil (O. *basilicum*), lemon basil (O. *americanum*) and sacred basil (O. *tenuiflorum*). The Greek and Turkish people tend to stick to cultivars of sweet basil (O. *basilicum*) and the Eastern Europeans and Africans grow sweet and sacred basil.

Most basils are annuals, and all should be treated as such in cool temperate climates. In tropical and subtropical regions, some basils, including sacred basil and lemon basil, are short-lived perennials. Thai basil has dark green, very aromatic leaves and purple stems and flower heads, while lemon basil has leaves with a distinct lemon scent, that are softly hairy, smaller and paler green than sweet basil. Sacred basil has soft, hairy leaves and pink flowers. Sweet basil grows to about 50 cm with oval-shaped leaves and white flowers.

Grow

Basil needs plenty of warmth and moisture. Propagate from seed, sown either inside or in a greenhouse; transplant seedlings outside after the last chance of frost is over. In warmer climates, perennial basils are easily grown from cuttings taken in spring or summer. Space plants about 40 cm apart. In colder regions, protect young plants in the first weeks with a plastic guard – cut the top and bottom from a plastic drink bottle and place this over the plant. Remove once the plant is established. When flowers appear, nip them back to encourage leaf growth. Basil grows best in rich fertile soils that are well drained. It needs full sun.

Garden talk

Basil leaves are often eaten raw in salads and dips. Basra adds basil to chilli and says that in Ethiopia, basil is used to flavour ghee. Fatima cooks basil with vegetables while Aesha adds it to spaghetti, usually mashed together with garlic first. Lemon basil can be fried with seafood and sacred basil has a sweet, spicy, pungent flavour and is used in salads and added to stir-fries and curries. Basils are also made into a fragrant tea that is used to treat coughs. Georgia says basil is good for headaches and to relax nervous people, and that if you drink it as a tea at night it will help you to sleep. She adds, 'Basil goes on any dish if you are using garlic and tomato.' The Greeks call this plant *vasilikós*.

GREEK RECIPE FROM GEORGIA

Pesto

3 cups fresh basil leaves
½ cup parsley
4 cloves garlic, peeled
½ cup olive oil
½ cup parmesan cheese, grated
½ teaspoon salt
½ cup pine nuts

Blend all ingredients together in a food processor or blender to form a paste.

Store in the refrigerator in a sealed container (it will keep for two weeks) or freeze.

Serve with other foods such as tiny boiled potatoes, vegetable soups, grilled tomatoes or pasta.

BEANS

Vicia sp., *Phaseolus* spp., *Lablab* sp. *and* Vigna *sp.*

Broad beans

Vicia faba

Broad beans are large, upright annuals, also commonly known as fava beans. They have pale green leaves, white, pink or red flowers and more or less hairy pods. The bean seeds are large, green or white, and flattened.

Grow

Plant seeds in autumn and winter directly into any reasonable, well-prepared soil to a depth of about 2 cm. Space the seeds 20 cm apart in rows 50 cm apart. Broad beans like full sun and compost or well-rotted animal manure dug into the soil before planting. Start harvesting young pods, to be eaten whole, after about two months. As the pods age they are harvested just for the beans inside the pod.

Broad beans

GREEK RECIPE FROM MARIA

Artichokes with Broad Beans

1.25 kg small broad beans
8–10 globe artichokes
1 cup onion, finely chopped
1 cup butter or oil
½ bunch dill, finely chopped
½ bunch parsley, finely chopped
1 bunch spring onions, chopped
1 teaspoon salt
½ teaspoon freshly ground black pepper
juice ½ lemon
2 teaspoons cornflour
2 teaspoons water

Egg and Lemon Sauce
2 teaspoons cornflour
½ cup milk
2 egg yolks, whisked
juice 1 lemon
reserved vegetable liquid
1 heaped teaspoon butter

Shell the broad beans (or shell half and leave half with shells, for added texture).

Prepare artichokes by cutting off the top half of the globe and discarding. Next trim off all the tough outer leaves until only soft, pale yellow-green leaves are left. Finally, remove most of the stalk and peel the remaining stalk with a vegetable peeler. Quickly place the prepared artichokes into a bowl of water with added salt and lemon juice, to prevent them from turning brown.

In a large saucepan, brown the onion slightly in the butter or oil. Add the broad beans, artichokes, dill, parsley, spring onions, salt, pepper and lemon juice. Mix the cornflour with the water to form a smooth paste, add to the saucepan along with enough water to just cover the vegetables and stir well.

Cover and simmer until vegetables are tender. Remove vegetables with a slotted spoon into a serving dish and keep warm. Reserve the liquid in the saucepan.

Egg and Lemon Sauce
Mix the cornflour with the milk. Pour the egg yolks into a small saucepan; slowly add the milk mixture, stirring well. Next add lemon juice to taste and ¼ cup of the reserved liquid. Stir over low heat until the mixture thickens, adding a little more of the vegetable liquid if too thick. Do not boil. Remove from heat and stir in the butter.

Pour the sauce over the vegetables and serve. **Serves 4.**

Garden talk

Broad beans are cooked as a vegetable by boiling or steaming, or can be added to stews, soups and stir-fries. They will also add nutrients to the soil if they are grown as a green manure crop and then dug back into the soil. Maria remembers planting broad beans under olive trees to add nutrients, while Fiona grows them in winter because they produce a lot for the space they take up.

BEANS

French beans

Phaseolus vulgaris

Runner beans

Phaseolus coccineus

French beans are also known as kidney beans and haricot beans and can have a dwarf or climbing habit. They are fast-growing annuals with green heart-shaped leaves and flowers that can be white, pink and purple. Bean pods vary enormously in texture and

French bean 'Purple King'

colour. Papery podded beans are grown for the dried bean seeds (kidney and haricot), those with leathery pods can be used whole when young or for the dried bean seeds when they are older while those with fleshy pods are grown for the whole bean (pod and seeds). Pod colour can be green, yellow and purple, while the seeds range in colour through black, white, red, brown, green and combinations of these.

Runner beans are perennials and are similar to the climbing French beans except that the pods are always green and more or less leathery, and flowers can be red as well as pink, white and mauve.

Grow

French and runner beans are planted in spring and early summer once the soil has started to warm up. Plant the seed into the garden where it is to grow in any reasonably rich well-drained soil, in full sun. Space dwarf varieties 10 cm apart in rows 30 cm apart, space climbing beans 15 cm apart in rows 75 cm apart. French beans are fast growing and self-pollinating, while runner beans need bees for pollination.

Garden talk

Julia boils her beans, whole or podded, in water with some corn, onions and pumpkin, adds a little salt and says it is bellisimo. Amy and Chitzu grow Purple King beans that turn green when they are cooked. The young tender beans of both French and runner beans are eaten raw or boiled, steamed, fried, marinated and pickled. Ripe, dried seeds are soaked and then boiled, baked, pureed and added to soups, dips, salads and many more dishes. For example, Kerama likes to cook dried beans on a low heat for a couple of hours, add some lentils and when cooked, drain and serve with lemon, salt and cumin or sometimes with butter and scrambled eggs.

GREEK RECIPE FROM SOPHIE
Fasolada (Bean Soup)

500 g dried beans (lima or butter)
1 cup olive oil
1 large onion, chopped
1 x 480 g tin chopped tomatoes
1 tablespoon tomato paste
2 medium carrots, sliced
½ cup celery, finely chopped
3 teaspoons salt
3 teaspoons freshly ground black pepper
1 hot chilli, finely chopped (optional)

Place the beans in a large bowl and cover with cold water to soak overnight. Next day, drain the beans, rinse them again in fresh water and drain again. In a 4 litre soup pot, bring the beans and 2 litres of water to the boil. Cover and lower heat to gently simmer. After an hour, add all other ingredients and continue to simmer until beans are tender and soft. Add extra boiling water if the soup becomes too dry. Time of cooking depends on the beans but is approximately 2 hours. **Serves 6.**

TURKISH RECIPE FROM HATICE
Green Beans with Tomato and Onion

1 kg fresh green beans
1 tablespoon olive oil
2 onions, diced small
1 teaspoon tomato paste
2–3 tomatoes, peeled and diced
1 teaspoon salt
¼ cup water
1 teaspoon sugar

Top and tail the beans and cut in half if small, or into thirds if large. In a large non-stick pot, add the olive oil, onions, beans and tomato paste. Cook, stirring, until onions are soft. Add tomatoes, water, salt and sugar and cook, covered, for approximately 45 minutes until beans are tender, stirring occasionally. Remove from heat and place in a container in the refrigerator. Serve cold as an accompaniment. **Serves 6–8.**

Hyacinth bean

Lablab purpureus

Hyacinth bean is a very vigorous perennial bean. It has both climbing and bush forms and in cold regions is grown as an annual. There are several varieties with varying leaf and flower colour. Leaves are dark-green or red-purple and flowers can be white, pink or purple and are fragrant. The pods are green or purple, curved and flattened with wavy margins. They contain three to five seeds.

Grow

Grow from seed sown in spring and harvest pods about four months later. Sow seed about 2 cm deep and 30 cm apart. Hyacinth beans like full sun and a reasonably fertile, well-drained soil. Train up a fence, trellis or tripod and keep well watered during dry weather.

Garden talk

Dried hyacinth bean seeds, young leaves and the swollen root are all eaten. Also immature pods and beans are boiled and eaten and are added to curries. These beans are never eaten raw as they contain a poisonous substance that is destroyed with cooking. Amy and Chitzu grow hyacinth beans up the outside fence and use the whole young pods in stir-fries.

Hyacinth bean

Joana's snake beans

Snake beans

Vigna unguiculata ssp. *sesquipedalis*

Snake beans have dwarf and climbing forms and are also known as asparagus bean and yard-long bean. Twining stems can be as long as 4 m. Yellow or mauve flowers grow on long stems and are followed by fleshy bean pods that can be green, yellow or a reddish-purple. Beans may grow as long as 50 cm but they are at their tastiest when about 25 cm. They are stringless.

Grow

These beans grow best in climates with warm summers where daytime maximums are 25°–35°C. Plant seeds about 2 cm deep into damp soil about 30 cm between plants. In cooler climates, plant in late spring and early summer, while in the tropics, plant from early spring to late summer. Climbing forms need trellises of about 2 m; as the young plants grow, train them up the vertical supports. Water regularly during dry weather. Start picking beans once they are about 20 cm long and before the seeds begin to swell.

Garden talk

Snake beans are grown mainly by the Asian gardeners. They taste similar to green beans, but the texture is more dense. The pods can be boiled, added to stir-fries or eaten raw. Joanna calls this bean *forei talin* and Edite and Joana like to use them in stir-fries. Some of the Chinese gardeners cut the beans into 3 cm lengths and stir-fry them with egg. Reddish-purple snake beans retain their colour when cooked. Leaves and young stems are also steamed and eaten as a vegetable.

Beetroots

Beta vulgaris

Beetroots

These root vegetables are biennials that grow as a clump of oval to lance-shaped leaves with a swollen root. If left in the ground, in the second year the plant will put up a flower stem to about 1 m topped with small green flowers. Swollen roots are usually bright red, but can be white or yellow or striped red and white.

Grow

Grow beetroots from seed sown directly into the soil where they are to grow from spring to late summer. Space seed 10 cm apart in rows 30 cm apart, thin the seedlings once the seeds have sprouted. Start harvesting roots about two months after planting. Beetroot grows well in any reasonable, well-drained soil in full sun. Make sure they have adequate water once the bulbs start to swell.

Garden talk

Both the leaves and roots of beetroot are eaten raw in salads. Take only the outside leaves, and don't take too many from each plant, or the roots will not develop. The roots are baked, boiled

ETHIOPIAN RECIPE FROM TAWFIK

Vegetable Salad

1 fresh beetroot, boiled until tender
1 large carrot, sliced and boiled until tender
2 hard boiled eggs
juice 1 lemon

Drain the beetroot and carrots. Plunge into cold water to cool quickly. Drain again.

Peel beetroot and slice. Peel eggs and slice. Arrange the beetroot slices on a plate, top with carrot slices, and then egg slices. Squeeze lemon juice over top and serve. **Serves 2.**

or steamed and eaten hot or cold. Kapitolina believes that beetroots, and beetroot juice, are fantastic for those who have stomach problems, like ulcers. Rawda uses beetroot in salads, after it has been boiled, and sometimes pickles it.

Bitter melon
Momordica charantia

Bitter melon plants are vigorous climbing vines with slender, five-angled stems. The large, lobed leaves can be 18 cm in diameter, and the male and female flowers are yellow and solitary. The unusual fruit has a warty skin that starts off pale green, then becomes dark green and finally turns yellow or orange when very ripe. The fruit can be long and tapering or pear-shaped.

Grow
These melons grow best where night-time minimum temperatures are 20°–25°C, but will tolerate lower temperatures particularly in the early stages of growth. They like well-drained, light, sandy soils with plenty of organic matter. Add manure to the soil about three weeks before planting. Plant only very fresh seeds, into individual pots, and keep in a warm place so that they are ready to be planted out, about 50 cm apart, once the weather is warm enough in late spring. Grow on a trellis about 2 m high. Water well during dry weather but don't over water. Fruit should be pale green, thick and juicy when harvested.

Bitter melon

Garden talk
Bitter melon has a strong, bitter flavour – the darker the skin the more bitter. It enhances the flavour of other ingredients but is something of an acquired taste. Mien says, 'Once you eat it you will like it so much, it doesn't make the meal too bitter.' She adds that you don't have to peel bitter melon, just cut and remove the seed.

VIETNAMESE RECIPE FROM MIEN

Bitter Melon Soup with Prawns

2 light green bitter melons
2 tablespoons rice
1 tablespoon vegetable oil
1 clove garlic, crushed
2 tablespoons pinkish white lemon grass stem, finely chopped
2 hot red chillies, seeded and finely chopped
4 cups water
2 tablespoons fish sauce
½ teaspoon sugar
250 g green prawns, peeled
2 spring onions, finely chopped

Slice bitter melons lengthwise, remove seeds with a spoon and discard. Finely slice the melons. Using a shallow tray, carefully grill the rice under a griller, stirring constantly, until golden brown. Grind the rice, with a mortar and pestle, to a fine powder.

Heat the oil in a stock pot. Add garlic, lemon grass and chillies and stir-fry until fragrant. Add water and bring to the boil. Add rice powder, fish sauce, sugar, bitter melon and prawns, cover, and simmer gently until prawns turn pink. Do not overcook. Spoon into bowls and garnish with spring onions. Serve immediately as this soup becomes much more bitter if reheated. **Serves 4.**

She likes to slice it very thin and fry it. It is also added fresh to salads, stuffed with rice and pork and baked, or simply boiled. To reduce the bitterness, rub cut slices of melon with salt, leave for ten minutes and then rinse well. The leaves and young stems are also eaten, usually stir-fried.

Bottle gourd, edible
Lagenaria siceraria

These vigorous, annual, climbing gourds have ribbed stems, large heart-shaped leaves, and single white flowers. Fruits vary from club- and bottle-shaped to round, with numerous variations in between, but they generally have pale green skin with mottled white patches. Edible bottle gourds most commonly seen in the gardens are long, round in cross-section and often slightly club-shaped. They are also known as the New Guinea bean.

Grow
Grow from seed sown from late spring to early summer. Seed germinates more rapidly if it is soaked for 12 hours first. Sow in groups of three where they are to grow, leaving about 1 m between plants. Thin to the strongest seedling. These plants will not tolerate frosts and do well in regions with warm, wet summers. They will grow in temperate regions but need to be kept well watered. Edible bottle gourds like a fertile, well-composted soil and full sun. They need some support or trellis.

Edible bottle gourd

PORK AND BAU SOUP

200 g pork fillet, thinly sliced
5 cups chicken stock
4 teaspoons fish sauce
¼ teaspoon salt
¼ teaspoon sugar
2 cups bau, peeled, seeded and thinly sliced
100 g bean curd, cut into 3 cm cubes
freshly ground black pepper
2 spring onions, thinly sliced
½ bunch coriander, chopped

In a 4-litre soup pot, combine pork and chicken stock. Bring to the boil, reduce heat and simmer for 10 minutes. Add fish sauce, salt and sugar and simmer a further 5 minutes. Skim surface if necessary. Add *bau*, cover and simmer for 10 minutes. Add bean curd and simmer a further 2 minutes. Add black pepper to taste. Serve garnished with spring onions and coriander. **Serves 4.**

STIR-FRIED PORK WITH BAU

300 g *bau*
200 g pork fillet, thinly sliced
1 tablespoon fish sauce
½ teaspoon sugar
½ teaspoon freshly ground black pepper
1 tablespoon vegetable oil
1 onion, sliced
2 cloves garlic, crushed
1 tablespoon soy sauce
1 tablespoon spring onions, chopped
½ bunch coriander leaves, chopped

Peel *bau*, cut in half lengthwise, remove and discard any seeds and thinly slice the flesh.

In a bowl, combine the pork, ½ tablespoon fish sauce, sugar and black pepper. Marinate for 30 minutes.

Heat oil in a non-stick frying pan or wok. Add onion and garlic and stir-fry until soft. Add pork and stir-fry 4 minutes. Add *bau*, soy sauce and remaining fish sauce. Stir-fry 3 minutes. Serve sprinkled with spring onion and coriander leaves. **Serves 2.**

Young fruit can be harvested once they are 10 cm long. Older fruit from some forms are still edible and are used in soups. These can be harvested any time.

Garden talk
Young fruits, 10–20 cm long, are eaten as vegetables or added to soup, stir-fried with pork or chicken, and fried together with eggs. Mien fries the leaves of edible bottle gourds which she calls *bau*, while So says, 'To eat it you first take the skin off and you slice it and you cook it with prawns or pork. It can also be peeled, sliced and steamed and then served with soy sauce.' He adds that you must always keep one *bau* for the seed.

CABBAGE FAMILY

Brassica spp.

This group of vegetables includes broccoli, cabbage, cauliflower, Chinese broccoli, Chinese cabbages, Ethiopian cabbage, kale and mustard greens. All are widely grown and used in the gardens.

Grow
All these plants like similar growing conditions. They are generally cool season crops that do best in rich loamy soils with lots of organic matter. They like full sun, moist soils, plenty of water during dry periods and are relatively frost-tolerant. Long summer days and high temperatures may cause the leaves to become tough.

Broccoli

B. oleracea Italica Group

Broccoli is an annual grown for its edible immature flower heads. It has typical cabbage leaves and flower heads usually in one central clump with some smaller clumps around the outside. The more usual type is green but there are also types with purple or white flower heads. Grow from seed sown into seed trays most of the year, transplant into rows 60 cm apart, with plants 40 cm apart. Different types need to be planted at, and will mature at, different times of the year.

Garden talk

Broccoli is grown by gardeners from many very different countries, including Russia, Chile and Ethiopia, but is used in similar ways. Immature flower heads, tender stems and young leaves are all eaten. They can be added raw to salads as well as being boiled, steamed, fried, marinated and served with white or cheese sauces. Broccoli is also added to soups, stews, casseroles and baked vegetable dishes.

Broccoli

CHILEAN RECIPE FROM AGUSTIN

PAN FRIED BROCCOLI

1 tablespoon oil
1 head broccoli, cut into florets
½ teaspoon dried oregano
½ teaspoon dried, ground cumin
¼ teaspoon salt
¼ teaspoon ground black pepper

Place oil and broccoli into a non-stick frying pan. Sprinkle with oregano, cumin, salt and pepper. Cover with a lid and gently fry over very low heat. After 20 minutes, turn broccoli over and continue to cook, covered, until tender. **Serves 2.**

Cabbage

B. oleracea Capitata Group

Cabbage is a biennial grown for its edible leaves which generally grow in a compact head. There are different types with rounded or pointed heads and leaf colours of pale green, dark green and red. The leaves can be crinkled or smooth. Grow from seed sown in seed trays from mid-winter to early autumn and transplanted into rows 50 cm apart with plants 30 cm apart. Start harvesting two months after sowing, but some cabbages can take up to 5 months to mature.

Garden talk

Although most gardeners grow non-heading types of cabbages, those that form a compact head are a favourite of gardeners from Eastern European countries. Leaves from these cabbages are eaten raw in salads and can be steamed, fried and boiled. They are also fermented to make sauerkraut and used to wrap other foods.

RUSSIAN RECIPE FROM LIOUDMILA

Cabbage Salad

200 g cabbage, finely chopped
100 g apples, cored and finely chopped
100 g celery, finely chopped
1 tablespoon olive oil
salt to taste

Toss all ingredients together in a bowl. **Serves 2.**

RUSSIAN RECIPE FROM ADELINA

Cabbage Rolls Stuffed with Vegetables

1 cabbage
½ cup basmati rice
1 tablespoon olive oil
3 onions, finely chopped
6 carrots, grated
½ bunch basil, finely chopped
bunch parsley, finely chopped
bunch dill, finely chopped
750 g minced beef
1 teaspoon salt
½ teaspoon freshly ground black pepper
2 teaspoons dill seeds
2 teaspoons ground hot Hungarian paprika
grated zest 4–5 lemons
chicken stock
3 sticks celery, finely chopped
125 g light sour cream
2 tomatoes, thinly sliced

Cut out the core of the cabbage and carefully separate and remove all the individual leaves. Cook in boiling, salted water until pliable but not cooked. Remove, drain and set aside. In another pot, bring water to the boil and half cook the rice (approximately 7 minutes). Drain and set aside. In a large frying pan or wok, add olive oil and gently fry onions until translucent. Add carrots, basil, half the parsley and half the dill and stir through. Add minced beef, rice, salt and pepper, dill seeds, hot paprika and lemon zest, and continue gently frying until mince is cooked. Place a portion of meat mixture on each leaf and fold carefully into rolls. When all the rolls are pre-pared, place them in a large pot and pour over the chicken stock until the level reaches 2–3 cm lower than the top of the cabbage rolls. Cover, bring to the boil, then turn heat to very low and cook gently for 1½ hours.

Add celery and sour cream to the pot. Place tomato slices in a layer on top of the cabbage rolls. Sprinkle with the remaining parsley and dill and cook gently, covered, for a further 10 minutes. **Serves 6.**

CABBAGE FAMILY

Cauliflower

B. oleracea Botrytis Group

Cauliflower is an annual or biennial plant grown for its immature flower head. Cauliflowers grow with short stems and a densely packed flower head that is surrounded and covered by the leaves. The flower head is usually white, but there are also green and purple types. Grow from seed sown in seed trays from late spring to the beginning of winter and transplant to rows 50 cm apart with plants 30 cm apart. Start harvesting small types after about three months, larger ones can take up to six months.

Garden talk

Only a few gardeners grow cauliflower, but most of those that do, eat the whole plant, not just the immature flower head. The flower heads are eaten raw in salads, or can be steamed, boiled, fried and pickled. They are added to soups, stews and sauces. Young leaves are eaten fresh and cooked, and flower-stalks and the mid-veins of the larger leaves are also cooked and eaten.

RUSSIAN RECIPE FROM ADELINA
Raw Cauliflower Salad

½ medium cauliflower
50 g dried large seedless raisins
mayonnaise

Soak raisins in cold water for 4–5 hours. Drain. Cut cauliflower into tiny florets. Toss together in a salad bowl. Add mayonnaise to taste and toss again. Let stand for 1 hour, tossing occasionally. Do not add salt or pepper. **Serves 2.**

CHILEAN RECIPE FROM AGUSTIN
Cauliflower Tortilla

½ cauliflower, cut into florets
2 eggs, beaten
½ teaspoon salt
½ teaspoon pepper
1 teaspoon dried oregano
1 teaspoon dried ground cumin
1 cup plain flour
1 tablespoon oil

Cook cauliflower in water until tender. Drain and puree. Mix beaten eggs, salt, pepper, oregano and cumin together. Combine with cauliflower. Stir in flour until mixture is firm. Heat a large non-stick frying pan on high until hot, then turn heat down to medium. Add oil, and when heated through, add mixture. Spread evenly over base of frying pan. Cook until browned and crisp. Cut into quarters then turn and cook other side to match. Can be served as is, or spread with toppings such as tomato, chilli and grated cheese and placed under griller until cheese melts. **Serves 2.**

CABBAGE FAMILY
Chinese broccoli

B. oleracea Alboglabra Group

Chinese broccoli is a fast-growing perennial with a single fleshy stem and dark green, rounded leaves. The leaves are usually darker green than those of Chinese flowering cabbage and flowers are white. Grow from seed sown into seed trays and then transplant so that there is about 15 cm between seedlings. Flowering heads are picked complete with stem and three to four young leaves just as the flowers begin to open. The more regularly the flowering heads are harvested the more will be produced. This broccoli differs from the more common European broccoli in having much

Chinese broccoli

smaller flower heads that are picked and cooked with the stem and young leaves.

Garden talk

Shu Xian loves to grow Chinese broccoli which she calls *gai lan*. The flower stalk, unopened flower buds and the tender leaves are all eaten, either whole or chopped. The fresh, slightly bitter flavour enhances soups, noodle and stir-fry dishes. The whole plant is high in calcium and iron. Joana uses this broccoli to make green soup; she says it is really a stew but she calls it a soup.

EAST TIMORESE RECIPE FROM JOANA

Green Soup

1 large bunch Chinese broccoli
2 large cloves garlic, finely sliced
1 onion, roughly chopped
5¼ cups good quality chicken stock
3 large potatoes, cubed
200 g chorizo sausage, sliced
350 g Polish sausage, sliced

Remove the tough lower ends of the broccoli stalks; then cut the broccoli into 5 cm pieces. Place broccoli, garlic and onion into a large pot and pour over the stock. Cover and simmer until tender. Remove from heat and puree in a food processor or blender. Return to pot and add potatoes and sausages. Cover and simmer until potatoes are cooked. **Serves 6.**

CABBAGE FAMILY

Chinese white cabbage

B. rapa Chinensis Group

Chinese white cabbage is a non-heading form of Chinese cabbage, often called *pak choi* or *bok choy*. It has thick, white, crisp leaf stalks and veins and glossy, smooth, broad, dark green leaves that form a loose cluster. There is a form with stems that are pale green instead of white, and leaves that are a paler green colour. Another type, known as Chinese flat cabbage, grows with glossy, very dark green, spoon-shaped leaves and white stems that lie flat on the ground. This type is more tolerant of hot weather than Chinese white cabbage. There are many different cultivars of all these cabbages. Grow them by sowing seed where it is to grow in spring or autumn. Thin so that there is about 25 cm between plants.

Chinese white cabbage

Garden talk

Young leaves and stems of these cabbages are eaten fresh in salads but they are also cooked in a wide range of dishes. Braised, steamed or simmered, the whole plant (except for the root) is served as a vegetable, sometimes accompanied by a white sauce. Amy and Chitzu grow *bok choy*. Amy tells us, 'We just wash it first and cut it, put it in the wok with oil and stir-fry. You can also boil it in soup, chicken soup or meat soup. Mostly we just cook it on its own, but we can add other things.' Chitzu adds laughing, 'Australians are more likely to add lots of things.' The flavour is delicate, mild and refreshing with a slight hotness.

Chinese flowering cabbage

B. rapa Chinensis Group

Chinese flowering cabbage is closely related to Chinese white cabbage, but like Chinese broccoli is grown more for its flower stems than its leaves. There are several different cultivars and it is best to grow the one suited to the local climate. This annual plant has oval fresh green leaves and yellow flowers. Sow seed in spring or autumn, where the plants are to grow and thin to about 10 cm between plants. Start harvesting after about 30 days, when the first flower buds begin to open. Pick the whole flowering stem with leaves and flowers.

Garden talk

Use young leaves in salads as well as young flower heads and open flowers. Roughly chop the stems and flower heads and steam, boil or fry. Older stems may need to be peeled. Mrs Poon calls this plant Chinese oily vegetables. 'You can put it into soup or you can fry it, but it doesn't taste so good when fried, I like it better put in soup. It is not hot or peppery, just mild like lettuce.' Be careful not to overcook it or the stems will lose their crispness. This cabbage is high in carotene, calcium and dietary fibre.

Chinese flowering cabbage

Chinese cabbage

B. rapa Pekinensis Group

Chinese cabbage is also called *bok choy* or *wong bok*. It grows with white, fleshy stems and broad, flat, light greenish-yellow, crinkled leaves. The leaves are erect and overlap to form a compact head. Over 200 different varieties are grown in China. Sow seed in late summer and autumn directly where they are to grow and thin to about 35 cm between plants. In the home garden, Chinese cabbage can be harvested at any stage, and young plants are useful 'cut and come again' vege-tables. To do this, cut the leaves leaving the very small central leaves. The plant will continue to grow from these.

Garden talk

This cabbage has a sweet flavour and crisp texture quite different to Euro-pean cabbages. Leaves are chopped and used in salads, stir-fries and soups, or just cooked as a vegetable. Never over-cook or the flavour will be destroyed. The leaves are also used to wrap other ingredients.

CABBAGE FAMILY

Ethiopian cabbage

B. carinata

Ethiopian cabbage is an annual that grows to over 1 m with purple tinged, branched stems and lobed leaves. Grow it from seed sown in late winter and spring, either in seed trays or where it is to grow. Transplant or thin to about 30 cm between plants. Start harvesting leaves as soon as they are large enough.

Garden talk

Young stems and leaves are added to salads while older leaves and stems are steamed or boiled. Immature flower heads can also be eaten like broccoli. Fatima calls this plant *rafu* and cooks it in the same way as spinach or silver beet. 'It gets quite big; we pick it before it flowers.' It is also known as *gommen* and Ethiopian mustard.

Ethiopian cabbage

CABBAGE FAMILY

Kale

B. oleracea Acephala Group

Kale is an annual or perennial that grows as a loose clump of typically cabbage leaves that do not form a solid head. Leaves can be green or purple. Grow from seed sown where it is to grow at any time of year and thin to about 50 cm between plants. Harvest leaves as soon as they are large enough to use.

Garden talk

Kale leaves are eaten fresh in salads when young, or can be boiled, steamed and fried. They are also added to soups and used to wrap other ingredients. Zeyneb calls the kale she grows Turkish or black cabbage. 'It is grown more in the Black Sea region of Turkey and the folk there have it as their favourite food, besides fish. We use it for *dolma*.' (See Zeyneb's recipe for silver beet dolmas, page 143. Kale leaves can be substituted for the silver beet leaves in this recipe, the only difference is that the kale leaves will need to be blanched first.)

Mustard greens

B. juncea

Mustard greens

Mustard greens grow to over 1 m with large, bright green leaves that taper towards the stem. The flowers are pale yellow and are followed by long, narrow seedpods containing reddish-brown seed. There are a large number of cultivars that vary in leaf shape and size. Plant seed where they are to grow at any time of year. Thin to about 30 cm between plants. Harvest outside leaves, leaving the rest of the plant to continue growing.

Garden talk

This leafy mustard is hot and tangy. It is high in vitamins A, B and C as well as iron and potassium. Joana tears up the big leaves and fries them. She calls them *mustarda* and says they are very good. Mai, Chue and Mor call this plant *xua jua* (*xua* meaning vegetable and *jua* meaning greens). They cook it with oil, salt and chilli, just stir-frying very quickly. Mor adds, 'You can cook it in many, many dishes. With pork soup, chicken soup, you can stir-fry, mix with meat, we also boil it and have it plain.' Fresh, young leaves are also added to salads.

EAST TIMORESE RECIPE FROM ANA

Stir-Fried Mustard Greens

2 teaspoons vegetable oil
1 clove garlic, crushed
1 cup mustard greens, washed, dried and torn into bite sized pieces

In a non-stick frying pan or wok, heat oil and add garlic. Stir-fry until fragrant and slightly coloured. Add mustard greens and stir-fry quickly until wilted. Serve immediately. **Serves 2.**

Canna, edible

Canna indica

Edible canna

This tropical plant grows to more than 2 m with elongated, oval, green leaves that can be 60 cm long and 30 cm wide. Flowers are bright red to orange and very decorative. Its roots are thick rhizomes that grow large, rounded, edible tubers. *C. indica* 'Purpurea' has dark green and purple leaves and red flowers. It is also called Queensland arrowroot.

Grow

Edible canna likes full sun but will tolerate some shade. Grow by separating underground rhizomes and planting out with at least two growth buds. Completely bury the rhizome and leave at least 60 cm between plants. Edible canna will grow in low nutrient soils and doesn't need much water, although roots are larger and more succulent if the plant is regularly watered. Harvest tubers in autumn when the leaves can be cut back to just above the ground. In cooler regions it dies back in winter.

Garden talk

The Vietnamese gardeners call this root *cu choi*, which means banana root. In North Vietnam, large areas of canna are grown to extract starch from the tubers. The starch is then used to make high-grade transparent starch noodles. Young shoots are also eaten and the leaves used to wrap food when baking. Canna tubers contain starch and sugar, as well as protein and potassium and smaller amounts of calcium and phosphorus. Tubers are dug, washed and eaten raw, or they can be boiled, baked or added to soup.

Capsicum and Chilli

Capsicum spp.

Capsicums and chillies all came originally from Central and South America, where they are still widely cultivated. They are in the *Capsicum* family but belong to about ten different species. Most of the sweet capsicums are in *C. annum* Grossum Group while the hot or chilli peppers are mostly in *C. annum* Cerasiforme Group and Longum Group as well as *C. frutescens*. The chillies grown by the Chilean gardeners are probably cultivars of *C. baccatum*. Most capsicums and chillies grow on branched shrubs that can be 1–2 m in height. They are annuals or short-lived perennials. Some are even climbers. The stems are woody at the base, while the leaves are glossy, dark green and an elongated heart shape. Small greenish-white flowers are followed by black, purple, green, orange, yellow or red fruit. Capsicums are generally larger with sweet flesh, while chillies are smaller with flesh that ranges from mildly hot to very hot.

Long sweet tapering capsicum
Bird's eye chilli

Grow

Grow capsicum and chilli bushes from seed sown in spring into seed trays. Transplant once the seedlings are big enough to move – generally about eight weeks later. These plants like full sun, and a well-drained soil with added animal manure, and they need long periods of hot weather. Plants are cold and frost-tender, so in cold regions they are all grown as annuals. In warm regions, they can be grown all year round, and C. *frutescens* cultivars will grow for many years and develop into substantial bushes. Prune these types once a year (generally in winter) and feed regularly. Harvest capsicum when they are sweet and ripe. Most start green but eventually turn red. Chillies can be harvested at any stage of development, but as a rule the longer they are left and the redder they are, the hotter they are.

Garden talk

Capsicums and chillies of different colours have different flavours and fragrances so they are not always interchangeable in recipes. They are rich in vitamins A and C.

Capsicums are eaten fresh in salads and can be grilled, roasted, baked, boiled and fried. They are particularly nice when stuffed. Shu Xian grows a small sweet capsicum that is perennial, while Georgia grows different varieties of capsicum, a sweet yellow one, a red one and a green one. She likes to grill and then peel them and put them in a bowl with oil, garlic and vinegar.

Chillies are added to sauces, soups and stews as well as curries. They are also made into dipping sauces and spice mixes, and finely sliced they are used as a garnish. Dried chillies can be pickled or steeped in oil. Agustin says, 'In

---

CHINESE RECIPE FROM AMY

Stir-Fried Chilli Chicken

350 g fresh whole mild, long green chillies
500 g minced chicken
1½ teaspoons salt
4 teaspoons Chinese cooking rice wine
5 teaspoons light soy sauce
2 tablespoons peanut oil
2 cloves garlic, crushed
2 teaspoons sugar
2 teaspoons sesame oil

Cut chillies in half lengthwise, remove seeds and cut into strips. Combine chicken with ½ teaspoon salt, rice wine and 2 teaspoons of soy sauce in a bowl. Heat peanut oil in a large wok or frying pan, over high heat. Add garlic, chillies and remaining salt and stir-fry briefly. Add chicken mince and stir-fry 2 minutes. Add sugar and the remaining soy sauce and stir-fry until most of the liquid has evaporated. Add sesame oil and stir-fry 1 minute. **Serves 2.**

GREEK RECIPE FROM SOPHIE

Fried Capsicum and Eggplant with Tomato Sauce

7 tablespoons of olive oil
3 large onions, finely chopped
5 cloves garlic, finely chopped
1 x 810 g can tomato chunks
800 g fresh tomatoes, chopped
2 tablespoons bottled mustard sauce
2 heaped tablespoons parsley, finely chopped
2 teaspoons salt
2 teaspoons freshly ground black pepper
2 teaspoons paprika
500 g sweet, long tapered yellow/green capsicums
1 kg Lebanese eggplants

To make the tomato sauce, in a large frying pan or pot, pour 4 tablespoons olive oil and gently fry the onions and garlic until browned. Add the canned tomato chunks and the fresh chopped tomatoes and stir constantly until well cooked. Add the mustard sauce, parsley, salt, pepper and paprika and stir until heated through. Set aside and keep warm.

Wash and dry the capsicums. Slice each eggplant lengthwise into 4 strips. In a large frying pan add the remaining olive oil and fry the capsicums whole, until browned. Set aside and keep warm. Fry the eggplant slices until browned and crisp, adding more olive oil if needed.

Serve the capsicums and eggplants hot, with the tomato sauce poured over the top, or mixed through. **Serves 6.**

spring I prepare the Chilean chilli; it is special because it is a very particular flavour. Somebody brought the seeds from Chile and it can last up to four years and then you have to really pull it out because it becomes too hot. The chilli is green, not big.' Vilma puts her chillies in vinegar and adds them fresh to salads. Thai adds chillies to fish sauce used for dipping while Amy and Chitzu grow a chilli that is only a little bit hot, and stir-fry it with chicken or pork. Shu Xian grows an unusual form of chilli that she has now had for more than two years. She says it is mild to hot. 'Stir-fry other vegetables and meat, put it in to enhance the taste of the whole dish. It depends on your ability to stand the hotness, you can put a half or a whole.' Hatice says that she doesn't use the hot ones but her husband loves them. 'Sabri eats them raw for breakfast and dinner.' Basra uses her chillies in two ways: either ground and cooked with meat sauce, or alternatively she crushes them in a blender with tomatoes, lemon, garlic and onion and then eats them. She also cooks the leaves. 'Wash them and then cut into very small pieces. Cut onion and fry in oil and then put tomato in and then it becomes a sauce and then put the leaves in and cook for about 15 minutes.' Fatima says that her chillies will survive the winter, they just cut them back and they come again. Tawfik likes very, very hot chillies; he chops them and uses them in salad as well as adding them to meat dishes. Kerama also uses a lot of chillies because they give a nice flavour to food. She likes to add them to salad with fetta cheese. Joana combines a few seeded and chopped chillies with crushed garlic, salt and lemon juice in a sealed jar, keeps it in the refrigerator and says these pickled chillies increase her appetite and give a lot of pleasure to anything she eats. Maria uses hot chillies when making a casserole or bean soup and Sophie says that chillies are good for immunity when viruses are going around. Oscar eats chillies in everything, even his breakfast, and he made a spray out of chillies to get rid of whitefly, possums and birds that were eating his produce.

AUSTRALIAN RECIPE FROM COREY
Tomato and Chilli Salsa

½ red capsicum, finely diced
1 small, very ripe, corn cob, kernels removed for use
1½ red chillies, seeded and finely chopped
2 heaped tablespoons fresh parsley, finely chopped
1 onion, finely chopped
4 fresh tomatoes, finely chopped
2 tablespoons lemon juice

Mix all ingredients together in a bowl and chill. Use as a topping for bruschetta, grilled meat or fish, or on baked potatoes.

EL SALVADOREAN RECIPE FROM JESUS
Purpusas

125 g mozzarella cheese, grated
125 g fetta cheese, grated or finely chopped
¼ onion, finely chopped
⅛ green capsicum, finely chopped
⅛ red capsicum, finely chopped
75 mL cream
250 g Mexican corn flour (*Masa Lista*)
400 mL water
¼ teaspoon salt
½ teaspoon olive oil

Make the filling by combining cheeses, onion, red and green capsicum and cream in a bowl.

In another bowl, stir the flour into the water and add the salt and olive oil. Knead well to make a moist but firm dough. Roll the dough into a log and cut into 8 equal portions. Roll each portion into a ball, then flatten and roll out until thin and round approximately 14–15 cm diameter. Place a generous heaped tablespoon of filling in the centre and fold over to form a semicircle. Seal edges together well.

Preheat a non-stick frying pan over medium heat and dry fry purpusas until browned (approximately 10 minutes). Turn over and cook until second side is browned (approximately 5 minutes). Serve immediately. **Makes 8.**

Carrots
Daucus carota Sativus Group

Carrots are biennials that grow with typically deeply divided green leaves in a dense clump with one long plump 'carrot' root to each clump. The edible roots are usually orange but can be red, white, yellow and even purple. In the second year, if the carrots are not harvested, strong upright leafy flower stems will grow from the centre of the clump with white or pink flowers.

Grow
All carrots like a sunny position and light well-drained soils without lumps or stones that might cause the roots to split. Add compost and well-rotted manure before planting, and water regularly. Grow carrots from seeds sown directly into the soil from September to February in rows 20 cm apart. Thin seedlings so that there is about 10 cm between each plant. Start harvesting young carrots after about two months.

Garden talk
Carrots are widely grown in the gardens because they don't take up a lot of space. They are eaten raw in salads or made into juice as well as being boiled, steamed, baked, fried and pickled. They are also added to soups, stews and casseroles. Basra grows carrots because they are one of the few vegetables she grew at home that she can also grow here while Rawda grows her carrots next to her coriander.

RUSSIAN RECIPE FROM LIOUDMILA
Mimosa Salad

6 hard-boiled eggs
6 potatoes, boiled and chopped
6 carrots, boiled and chopped
3 medium-size onions, finely chopped
300 g tasty cheese, grated
6 tablespoons mayonnaise

Separate the egg whites from the egg yolks and finely chop both. Using a dish with high sides, assemble the salad in layers.
   First layer, potatoes scattered with onions on top, and covered with 2 tablespoons mayonnaise.
   Second layer, carrots scattered with onions on top, and covered with 2 tablespoons mayonnaise.
   Third layer, cheese scattered with chopped egg whites on top, and covered with 2 tablespoons mayonnaise. Scatter final layer with chopped egg yolks and serve. **Serves 4–6.**

AFGHANI RECIPE FROM BASIRA
Ghabeli Poulou

4 large carrots, cut into matchsticks
1 tablespoon oil
200 g sultanas
1 tablespoon sugar
10 g almonds
10 g pistachio nuts
1 kg basmati rice
6 cups water
3 teaspoons salt
1 kg lamb, cut into strips
1 onion, chopped
½ teaspoon freshly ground black pepper

In a frying pan gently fry the carrots in the oil for 5 minutes. Add the sultanas and continue cooking until carrots are cooked. Add the sugar and take the carrot mix off the heat. Stir through the almonds and the pistachios and set aside to keep warm.
   Wash rice and drain well. In a large pot, add rice, 4 cups water and 2 teaspoons of salt. Gently bring to a simmer, cover with a lid and continue simmering, stirring occasionally until water has been absorbed and rice is cooked and fluffy.
   At the same time in another pot, simmer the lamb and onion in 2–3 cups water until cooked, stirring occasionally. Season with pepper and the remaining salt.
   Spoon the rice onto a large serving platter, top with lamb, and finally the carrot mixture. **Serves 6.**

Celery and Chinese celery

Apium graveolens

Celery is an erect biennial plant that can grow as tall as 1 m. It has a fleshy bulbous root, from which the familiar straight stems grow. The opposite leaves are mid-green and indented. Flowers are greenish-white and grow on stalks at the top of the plant. Chinese celery is similar but smaller with narrower stems.

Grow

Grow celery from seed sown in spring into any reasonable soil. Chinese celery will tolerate a greater range of conditions than common celery, but both like full sun and humus-rich, well-drained soils. Water well during dry weather as plants that have been allowed to dry out will have tough stems. Water occasionally with liquid seaweed fertiliser to promote green growth. Harvest stems when they are mature. Pick the leaves and young stems of Chinese celery as soon as plants are large enough to withstand harvest, and continue to harvest right through summer into autumn.

Garden talk

Succulent celery stems are eaten fresh in salads, and can be cooked in soups and stir-fries. Shu Xian pours boiling water over either celery to kill any bacteria, then cuts the stems into small pieces. She adds water (about one glass full to four pieces of celery) and puts this in the blender. 'After that I strain it and put a little bit of honey and lemon juice. It is a beautiful taste. You can use stems and leaves. I drink it for my health and to improve my veins and to reduce high blood pressure and for digestion.' Tju Ing also uses celery for high blood pressure. 'Sometimes

Chinese celery in flower

CHINESE RECIPE FROM EDITE

Minced Pork with Chinese Celery

2 tablespoons of peanut oil
4 cloves garlic, crushed
½ teaspoon salt
1 bunch Chinese celery, leaves and stems, chopped into 5 cm lengths
200 g minced pork
125 mL chicken stock
1 tablespoon light soy sauce
1 teaspoon sugar

In a non-stick frying pan or wok, heat oil, add garlic and salt, and stir-fry briefly. Add celery and pork, and stir-fry until pork is browned (breaking up any large lumps). Add chicken stock, soy sauce and sugar, and stir-fry until most of the liquid has evaporated. **Serves 2.**

when I have an argument with my husband my blood pressure goes up and I will eat some celery.' Vilma makes celery tea that she says is good for people who are tired, while Sitina uses celery in soup, the whole lot, leaves and stem. Chinese celery is grown as much for its leaves as its stems. Its flavour is much stronger than ordinary celery. Add a few leaves or finely chopped stems to salads, soups, stews, stir-fried rice and noodles. Stems can be stir-fried on their own, with a little soy sauce and sesame seeds. Ruyet says that Chinese celery was grown in the south of Vietnam, not the north, and that initially northerners couldn't stand the smell of it. 'Now everyone eats it. Wash it, chop it and then you can fry it with calamari, prawn or beef.' Tai says that it is good for high blood pressure, either eaten raw or fried with beef.

Chicory
Cichorium intybus

Red chicory

Chicory has a long taproot, topped by an upright rosette of large leaves. Tall flowering stalks up to 1 m grow from this rosette, and bear dandelion-like blue flowers. Chicory is also known as Italian bitter lettuce

Grow
Chicory grows easily from seed sown in spring into seed trays, with seedlings transplanted when still small. It will grow in most soils and likes full sun and adequate water during dry periods to keep the leaves fresh and crunchy.

Garden talk
Young leaves are used in salads, added to stir-fries and cooked by steaming or boiling. The roots are used as a coffee substitute or added to coffee. Maria says that chicory is very bitter. 'It is very good for you and you can drink the water after you boil the leaves. It is good for the blood.'

GREEK RECIPE FROM GEORGIA

FRICASSEE

2 tablespoons butter
1 large onion, chopped
1 kg boneless lamb, cubed
1 cup chicken stock
2 tablespoons parsley, chopped
1 teaspoon dill, finely chopped
1 teaspoon salt
1 teaspoon freshly ground black pepper
2 heads endive, washed well, trimmed of any coarse outer leaves, and cut in half
2 heads firm, small chicory (eg. Treviso or Radicchio), washed well and quartered
extra parsley and dill

Egg and Lemon Sauce
Up to 1½ cups chicken stock
1 tablespoon cornflour
3 eggs, separated
zest of 1 lemon
1 teaspoon salt
1 teaspoon freshly ground black pepper

In a large saucepan, melt butter and gently fry onion until translucent. Increase heat and add cubed lamb. Cook, stirring, for approximately 2 minutes until meat juices have evaporated. Meat should not brown. Reduce heat and add stock, herbs and salt and pepper to taste. Cover and simmer gently for 1½ hours.

Add prepared endive and chicory and continue to cook until tender. Drain liquid from pan into a measuring jug. Keep saucepan contents warm while making the sauce.

Egg and Lemon Sauce
Make the reserved liquid up to 1½ cups with chicken stock. Pour into a saucepan and bring to the boil. Mix cornflour with a little cold water to form a paste and add to the stock, stirring until thickened. Boil for 1 minute.

In a bowl, beat egg whites until stiff, add egg yolks and continue beating until light and fluffy. Add lemon zest. Gradually pour the stock into the egg mixture, beating constantly. Return sauce to saucepan and cook, stirring over low heat for 1–2 minutes to cook egg. Do not let sauce boil. Remove from heat and continue stirring for 1 minute. Season with salt and pepper.

Pour the sauce over lamb and vegetables, cover and keep warm for 5 minutes. Serve sprinkled with chopped extra parsley and dill. **Serves 4.**

Chinese boxthorn

Lycium barbarum

Chinese boxthorn grows as a small tree of about 2 m with long arching branches. It has mid to dark green, small, oval leaves, mauve flowers and small elongated, orange or red berries. Most forms have thorns but some do not.

Grow
This plant grows easily from seed and has become a weed of waste ground in many regions of the world, growing from berries dropped by birds. Sow seed in spring in any well-drained soil in full sun. It can also be grown from cuttings taken in autumn or spring.

Chinese boxthorn

Harvest berries in autumn, and leaves any time of the year.

Garden talk

Leaves are slightly bitter and are used fresh or dried as a flavouring, added to pork dishes and a range of soups. Mrs Poon uses the leaves in chicken soup. 'It is good for your eyes, you will see brighter, better.' Leaves are added to rice while it is cooking to give the rice a pleasant aromatic flavour. The small berries have a sweet anise flavour and are high in carotene. In China, they are added to important ceremonial dishes, especially those with chicken or duck. Both the leaves and berries are made into a tea that is regarded as a tonic. Shu Xian also grows Chinese boxthorn and says that it can be used for medicinal reasons, as well as in cooking.

Coriander

Coriandrum sativum

Coriander

This erect annual herb grows to about 40 cm with lower leaves that are rounded and lobed, while the upper leaves are linear and finely dissected. Pale pink flowers are followed by seed that are small green berries, which become brown and ridged when ripe.

Grow

Grow coriander from seed sown in spring or autumn. Plant the seed where it is to grow because it does not transplant well. Thin to about 15 cm between plants. In areas with hot, dry summers, coriander is best planted in autumn so it does not go straight to seed. Coriander does well in any good, nutrient-rich soil that is well drained. In very hot regions it can be grown in the shade, but in cooler regions grow it in full sun. Keep well watered. Leaves have the best flavour while the stems are still soft and before the flowers start to form. Whole plants are harvested for their roots at the same time. Pick seed as they start to turn from green to brown.

Garden talk

Coriander is a nutritious herb rich in calcium, phosphorus, beta-carotene and vitamin C. It has an unusual, very

IRANIAN RECIPE FROM AGHDAS

Cookou Sabzi (Herb Omelette)

200 g fresh herbs (coriander, chives, garlic, spring onion, parsley), chopped
5 eggs
1 tablespoon plain flour
1 teaspoon salt
1 teaspoon freshly ground black pepper
extra spice, either 2 fresh chillies, finely chopped or 2 teaspoons ground cinnamon
¼ cup oil

Beat all ingredients together, except the oil. In a non-stick frying pan add half the oil, and heat. Pour half the mixture into pan. Cook on one side, turn, and cook on the other side. Remove and keep warm. Add remaining oil to pan and heat. Cook remaining mixture in the same way. Serve with rice. **Serves 2.**

strong taste when fresh, and both the leaves and roots are commonly used in Asian cooking. Leaves are used as garnish and to add fragrance to salads, soups, meat dishes and particularly fish dishes. Marcos adds coriander to soup, while Tawfik says that he always grows coriander and uses it in salad. 'If there is no coriander in the salad then it doesn't taste any good. I like coriander very much.' Mai, Chue and Mor add coriander leaves when they stir-fry meat but say that they never use the roots. The dried seed has a sweet, almost orange, taste and is an important ingredient of most curry spice mixes. The flavour of the seeds is enhanced if they are lightly cooked in a dry frying pan and then crushed just before they are to be used.

CHILEAN RECIPE FROM AGUSTIN

Pebre a la Chilena (salsa)

1 hot chilli, finely chopped
20 g fresh coriander leaves and stems, finely chopped
1 small onion, finely chopped
1 clove garlic, finely chopped
1 large tomato, finely chopped
½ teaspoon ground cumin
1 teaspoon dried oregano
¼ teaspoon ground pepper (black or white)
¼ teaspoon salt
½ cup boiling water
olive oil

Place chilli, coriander, onion, garlic and tomato in a bowl. Add seasonings and boiling water. Stir well. Place the mixture in a glass jar with a lid. Cover with plenty of olive oil. Place jar in refrigerator and keep for a couple of days, then use with cooked meats.

Corn (maize)

Zea mays

Corn is an annual grass that can grow to 4 m with strong upright stems and long, arching lance-shaped leaves. Male flowers are erect spikelets at the top of the plant; female flowers grow in the leaf axils. Corn kernels can vary in colour from white, yellow, red, purple and blue or combinations of all of these.

Grow

Grow corn from seed sown directly into the garden bed from spring to early summer after the last chance of frost. Space plants 20 cm apart in rows 80 cm apart. Corn likes full sun and a humus-rich well-drained soil. Add compost and manure before planting. Start harvesting about three months after planting.

Garden talk

'Sweet' corn grown for its sweet kernels can be eaten fresh, boiled, steamed, roasted and fried. It is also delicious

Sweet corn

added to soups and stir-fries. Agustin says that the corn grown in Chile has very big cobs, is yellow-green in colour and the kernels are big too and look like horse's teeth. Jesus explains that they call their 'sweet' corn *elote* and that it is different from the dry corn used to make flour. Tawfik planted his corn right around the edge of his garden. He likes to roast his corn on charcoal. 'Remove the leaves and then put it on the charcoal. It will make it very nice, beautiful.' He also likes to remove the kernels from the cob and cook it in a very hot pan with a little salt. Ana boils the corn but adds that she also likes to peel the cob and then cook it with beans, meat, chilli, basil, lemon and garlic.

Other corns contain more starch and less sugar than 'sweet' corn and are used mostly to produce flour or meal, for making bread, cakes, polenta, tacos,

Dolphin's corn

tortillas and tamales. Dolphin, of all the gardeners, is the most passionate about corn. 'All the time I grow corn, like I say to you corn is the best, if you have cancer you can destroy it. If you eat a lot of corn you can't get cancer. This is different corn. The corn is different colours, it tastes better, stronger, very

CAPE VERDEAN RECIPE FROM DOLPHIN
CACHUPA

750 g white maize (corn) grits
750 g dried borlotti beans
4 litres water
2 tablespoons olive oil
1 litre chicken stock
1 smoked pork hock
500 g lean salt pork meat (bacon in the piece)
400 g fresh uncooked chorizo sausage
250 g blood pudding sausage
1 tablespoon ground black pepper
1 whole bulb garlic, each clove peeled and crushed
4 tomatoes, chopped
4 bay leaves
½ large pumpkin, peeled and diced
4 cassava roots, peeled and chopped (available frozen)
1 onion, finely chopped
4 teaspoons chicken stock powder

Wash and drain the maize grits and the borlotti beans. Place in large 8–10 litre preserving pan and add water, 1 tablespoon olive oil and chicken stock. Bring to the boil. Add smoked pork hock and salt pork meat, partially cover with lid, and lower heat to maintain a steady but slow boil. Cook for 1 hour, then add chorizo sausage and blood pudding sausage (leave both whole), and continue to cook, partially covered, for a further 1½ hours. During this time, check that liquid always covers the ingredients; otherwise add a little more water.

Next add pepper, garlic, tomatoes and bay leaves, and continue cooking for a further hour. Add pumpkin and cassava and cook for a further ½ hour. If mixture looks too dry, add a little more boiling water. At the same time, in a frying pan, add remaining olive oil and gently fry the onion. Add this to the pot together with chicken stock powder.

Remove pork hock, salt pork, chorizo sausage and blood pudding sausage with a slotted spoon or tongs, cut into small pieces, and return to the pot. Check seasonings and, if necessary, add a little salt and pepper to taste. Remove from heat and let *cachupa* stand, covered, for at least 20 minutes before serving to allow flavours to be absorbed. **Serves approximately 20.**

Any leftover *cachupa* freezes well in small containers. It can also be fried with onions until dry or almost crispy on the bottom and served as a very sustaining breakfast.

sweet but hot as well. I make a very special dish with the corn, from my country, called *cachupa*. If you eat it in the morning, you stay all day and you no need to eat, keep you, you never become fat.' The corn that Dolphin grows is one of the high starch, low sugar types so that it is quite 'dense' and very filling.

Cress

Lepidium sativum

Cress

Cress is a quick growing erect annual with deeply divided, dark green leaves and white to mauve flowers. There are also cultivars with broader and curled leaves.

Grow
Grow from seed sown through most of the year except summer. Resow every few weeks to maintain a constant supply. Cress needs full sun or semi-shade but must have nutrient-rich soil and plenty of water if the leaves are to be succulent and not too bitter.

Garden talk
Cress is added to salads, sandwiches, soups and any other dish where the hot, peppery flavour enhances the taste. Zeyneb loves her cress which she says is Turkish rocket, she calls it *tere*. She says that everyone wants to try it and that everybody likes the taste. 'In Lebanese bread, you put this one inside and little bit of white cheese and you roll it up, it is beautiful. Cheese and rocket roll.' Fatima calls this plant *rashad* and uses it in salads. The fresh or dried seeds and seedpods are eaten and in Ethiopia, an oil is made from the seeds.

A Lebanese type cucumber

Cucumber

Cucumis sativus

Cucumbers are usually annual plants that have rough, hairy stems trailing over the ground with large oval, lobed leaves and male and female flowers. The fruits are very variable and can be white, green and/or yellow skinned, smooth, hairy, warty or with spines. The fruits are generally longer than they are wide, but some varieties like Crystal Apple are ball-shaped.

Grow

Grow from seed sown directly into the garden bed in late spring and early summer. Space plants about 1 m apart. Climbing varieties can be grown up a trellis or tripod. Cucumbers do best in humus-rich soil in full sun. Sweet, crisp fruit need plenty of water during dry weather.

Garden talk

Cucumbers are usually eaten fresh in salads and sandwiches, or made into dips. Zeyneb grows cucumbers and loves to share them with her neighbours. 'I give some to everybody, I have plenty.' Rawda grew her cucumber seeds in small containers and then transplanted them into the garden. Vicki adds cucumbers to salads or just eats them on their own. Cucumbers can also be lightly cooked; Edite fries cucumber with shredded pork and Tju Ing uses them in sweet and sour recipes.

AUSTRALIAN RECIPE FROM COREY
Cucumber Dip

1 cucumber, grated and squeezed dry
½ teaspoon salt
½ teaspoon freshly ground black pepper
1 small tub low fat, natural yoghurt
2 cloves garlic, crushed
½ onion, finely chopped
¼ cup parsley, finely chopped
¼ cup mint, finely chopped
¼ cup coriander, finely chopped
½ teaspoon ground cumin

Mix all ingredients together in a bowl and chill. Serve with toast, crudités, or with a curry.

Dandelion

Taraxacum sect. *Ruderalia* spp.

Dandelion is a perennial that grows as a circle of deeply toothed, lance-shaped, bright green leaves. Leafless hollow purplish stems grow from the centre of the clump and are topped by a single golden-yellow flower. Dandelions flower right through the year and carry a rich supply of nectar that is popular with bees and many other insects. The flower is followed by a ball of silky, white, plumed seeds.

Dandelion

Grow

Dandelion is an extremely common and invasive weed often found in gardens, lawns and waste ground. Grow from seed planted in spring or dig up wild plants and replant into the garden. Harvest the leaves when needed and the roots in autumn.

Garden talk

Dandelion leaves contain potash, taraxcin and vitamins A and C, while the roots provide copper and iron. The whole plant is detoxifying and aids in the removal of waste from the body. Lioudmila uses dandelion flowers in jam, leaves in salad and dried and powdered roots for tea. Kapitolina rubs the sap from the flower stem onto bites while Vicki adds the leaves to pasta sauces and Fiona blanches the leaves and adds them to salads.

Spring Aroma Salad

50 g dandelion leaves
50 g young stinging nettle leaves, blanched
75 g parsley
25 g sorrel
1 apple, peeled and quartered
1 hard-boiled egg, peeled
2 walnuts, crushed
½ teaspoon salt
¼ teaspoon freshly ground black pepper
3 teaspoons mayonnaise

Wash and dry the herbs and then chop them finely. Grate the apple. Mash the hard-boiled egg. Mix all of these and the walnuts together in a bowl. Add salt, pepper and mayonnaise, and toss well. Let stand several hours in the refrigerator before serving, to bring out the flavours. **Serves 6.**

Lioudmila says that this salad helps to preserve the body's energy.

Dill
Anethum graveolens

Dill

Dill is a tall annual herb that grows to over 1 m. The single stem has many feathery blue-green leaves and is topped in summer by clusters of small yellow flowers. These are followed by flat, oval brown seeds that will self-sow readily.

Grow
Grow dill from seed sown where the plants are to grow, as seedlings do not transplant well. Sow seed in spring and summer and thin to about 30 cm between plants. Successive plantings are needed to maintain a supply of fresh foliage. Dill likes full sun and rich, fertile soil with lots of organic matter. Keep well watered during dry weather. Seed heads are harvested just as the seed starts to turn brown.

Garden talk
Both the leaves and seeds are used in cooking and medicine. The seeds aid digestion by easing stomach-aches that are caused by wind. Dill water is often given to children to relieve colic. The leaves have a distinct, pleasant flavour and are best used fresh. Add leaves to fresh cucumber and yoghurt as a side dish and sprinkle chopped leaves over any dish containing lamb, just before serving. Kapitolina adds dill leaves to soup and uses them as a garnish. She drinks tea, made by pouring boiling water over the seeds, to lower blood pressure.

GREEK RECIPE FROM SOPHIE
POTATO SALAD

4 large potatoes
1 carrot, diced
1 onion, finely chopped
3 small spring onions, finely chopped
2 tablespoons parsley, finely chopped
2 tablespoons dill, finely chopped

Dressing
⅓ cup olive oil
¼ cup lemon juice
1 tablespoon vinegar
1 teaspoon salt
1 teaspoon freshly ground black pepper

Wash the potatoes well and boil in water until softened. Drain and rinse under cold water, peel and dice into small pieces. Boil the carrot in water until softened. Drain and rinse under cold water. In a large salad bowl, mix together the potatoes, carrot, onion, spring onions, parsley and dill.

Dressing
Combine all the dressing ingredients in a large clean screw-top jar and shake well.

Pour the dressing over the salad, mix well, and leave for 2 hours to absorb the flavours. **Serves 4–6.**

Eggplant
Solanum melongena

Lebanese eggplant

Eggplants come in a variety of shapes (pea, golf ball, apple, egg, cigar), sizes and colours (red, white, purple, yellow, green and combinations of these), but those most commonly grown in the gardens are long, slender and purple or rounded and plump. All eggplants are short-lived perennials that are usually

GREEK RECIPE FROM GEORGIA
BRIUM (LAYERED VEGETABLE CASSEROLE)

500g eggplants
1kg zucchini
4 medium potatoes
1 green capsicum
1 red capsicum
4 medium tomatoes
2 large onions
1 x 425g tin chopped tomatoes
2 cloves garlic, crushed or finely chopped
1 tablespoon sugar
1 tablespoon dill, finely chopped
2 tablespoons tomato paste
2 tablespoons parsley, chopped
salt and pepper to taste
½ cup olive oil
250g fetta cheese, thinly sliced

Cut eggplants and zucchinis into approximately 2 cm slices. Peel potatoes and slice slightly thinner than the eggplants. Seed the capsicums and cut into rings. Slice tomatoes and onions. Mix together the tinned tomatoes, crushed garlic, sugar, dill and tomato paste.

Lightly oil a large baking dish. Arrange half the eggplants, zucchinis, potatoes, capsicum rings, tomato slices, onions and parsley in single layers. Season with salt and pepper. Cover with half the tomato mix.

Repeat layers of remaining vegetables. Season with salt and pepper and cover with remaining tomato mix. Pour olive oil over the top, cover with foil, and bake in a moderate oven (350°F / 180°C) for 1½ hours. Remove foil. Place sliced fetta cheese on top, and bake uncovered for a further 15–20 minutes, or until cheese melts a little. Serve cut into squares. **Serves 6–8.**

TURKISH RECIPE FROM HATICE
KARNI YARIK (STUFFED EGGPLANTS)

2 tomatoes
2 large eggplants
2 tablespoons olive oil
300 g minced beef
2 onions, diced
4 teaspoons tomato paste
½ bunch parsley, finely chopped
1 teaspoon salt
½ teaspoon freshly ground black pepper
small tomato and green capsicum wedges to serve
(optional)

Preheat oven to 400°F (200°C). Place tomatoes in a bowl, cover with boiling water and let stand for a short time. Drain and the skin will peel off easily, then dice.

Peel the eggplant skin in strips lengthwise, using a vegetable peeler, to give a striped presentation. Place the eggplants in a bowl of cold, salted water for 15 minutes. Drain and pat dry with paper towelling. Cut the eggplants in half, lengthwise. Heat 1 tablespoon olive oil in a non-stick frying pan and gently fry eggplants on both sides until browned. Scoop out centre flesh from cut sides and use at some other time in soup, dip or a vegetable mix.

Heat remaining olive oil in a non-stick frying pan or pot and gently cook mince, stirring occasionally, until browned and moisture has evaporated. Add onions and continue cooking until soft. Add tomato paste and diced tomatoes and cook for a further few minutes. Add finely chopped parsley, salt and pepper and cook, stirring, for a further 2–3 minutes. Remove from heat.

Stuff the eggplants with the meat mixture and place a tomato wedge and a green capsicum wedge on top of the stuffing. Place the eggplants in a baking dish and pour a glass of water into the bottom of the dish. Cover with foil and bake in the oven for 20–30 minutes until tender. **Serves 4**

grown as annuals. They grow as branched shrubs to 1.5 m with a woody base and hairy stems. Green leaves are softly hairy and flowers come in a range of purples.

Grow
Eggplants are grown from seed sown in spring. Plant out seedlings about 50 cm apart, after the last chance of frost, into well-prepared nutrient-rich soil in full sun. Water regularly because drought stress causes bitterness. Fruit should be shiny and firm with a good strong colour before harvesting.

Garden talk
Eggplants are sliced into stir-fries, casseroles or stews, or roasted whole or stuffed. In the gardens the long, white variety seems to be most popular amongst the Chinese, while Turks prefer the long purple types and Greeks the plump purple ones. Hatice uses her eggplants in many different meals and particularly likes to stuff them. Georgia grows the big plump purple eggplants but has also been trying to grow one from home that has a white skin with purple streaks. She likes to make eggplant dip by roasting whole eggplant until soft and then blending the eggplant flesh with garlic, onion, parsley, vinegar and salt.

Epazote
Chenopodium ambrosioides

Epazote

This tall annual plant grows with irregular branches and lance-shaped leaves to well over one metre. Small green flowers grow densely in flower heads in summer.

Grow

Grow from seed sown in spring directly where the plants are to stay, in any reasonable, well-drained soil in full sun. Harvest leaves as soon as the plants are big enough.

Garden talk

Fresh or dried leaves are used to flavour bean, vegetable (especially mushroom) and fish dishes. Adding leaves to bean dishes is believed to reduce flatulence. A pleasant tasting tea, often called Mexican tea, is made from the leaves. Heriberto calls this plant *paico* and says it is very good for stomach-aches. 'You boil the leaves and then put a little bit of sugar and when your stomach is very cold, and your stomach-aches, you just drink it.' Julia also uses *paico* for stomach-aches.

Fennel
Foeniculum vulgare

Fennel

Fennel is an extremely hardy perennial that grows up to 2 m in height, has strong stems and feathery, yellow-green leaves. The tiny, yellow flowers grow at the top of the plant and are followed by light brown, flat, ribbed seeds. There is a bronze form of fennel and another form known as Florence fennel that develops a white bulbous base.

Grow

Propagate all fennels from seed sown in spring where the plants are to grow. Thin to about 40 cm between plants. Fennel will self-sow readily once established, and is a declared noxious weed in some regions. It grows best in full sun in a light, well-drained soil. Pick

GREEK RECIPE FROM GEORGIA

SPANAKOPITA (GREEK GREENS AND CHEESE PIE)

1 kg mixed leafy greens (from fennel leaves, spinach,
parsley, silver beet, nettles, dandelion, plantain, sorrel)
7 eggs
125g fetta cheese
125g ricotta cheese
1 onion, chopped
1 clove garlic, crushed
olive oil
salt and pepper
dried oregano
60g butter
500g filo pastry

Wash leafy greens, dry and place in a large bowl. Tear
into small pieces and sprinkle heavily with salt, rubbing it
into the leaves. Rinse salt off thoroughly and drain.

Beat the eggs in a separate bowl. Crumble in the fetta
and add the ricotta.

Gently fry onion and garlic in a little olive oil until
translucent. Add to greens. Pour in the egg and cheese
mixture. Combine well and season to taste with salt,
pepper and oregano.

Butter a large, deep baking dish (23cm x 33cm approximately). Melt remaining butter in a small saucepan.
Place 1 sheet of filo in dish and brush with melted butter.
Repeat with each layer of filo, turning each sheet so that
it is not all piled directly on top of each other – brushing
each layer with butter and letting the filo hang over the
sides of the dish. Continue until 3 sheets of filo are left.

Pour in the filling and fold the pastry edges in over the
top. Place the remaining sheets on top, brushing each
with melted butter. Make two or three slits with a knife
in the top layers of filo down to the filling to act as steam
vents. Bake at 375°F (190°C) for 50 minutes. Cut into
squares and serve with a Greek salad (see page 133).
Can also be eaten cold the next day. **Serves 8.**

leaves at any time, and harvest seeds
in autumn by cutting off the seed heads
as the first seeds begin to turn brown.

Garden talk

The seeds, stems and leaves, as well as
the bulbous base of Florence fennel, are
all edible with a delicious anise flavour
and scent that combines particularly
well with fish. Dry roasted fennel seeds
are chewed as a breath freshener,
handed around at the end of the meal.
Georgia uses fennel seeds for stomach
complaints and the leaves to make
spanakopita while Vicki adds fennel,
which she calls *maratho*, to tomatoes,
rice and mince meat and says it is a
very tasty dish. She also boils the roots
to make a tea to help the kidneys. She
says to put some roots in 3 litres of
water and boil it until there is only 1½
litres left and then drink it, hot or cold,
when it is needed. Rawda flavours okra
and molokhia with fennel, which she
calls *shamar*.

Fish plant

Fish plant

Houttuynia cordata

Fish plant is low and spreading with
leaves that are pointed and heart-
shaped, and range in colour from
green to cream, pink, yellow, red and
blue-green in various combinations on
different cultivars. The flowers are
white with a bright yellow centre
spike.

Grow

This herb is best grown by dividing old plants in autumn or spring. Plant in a semi-shaded position in any reasonable soil, although it does best in damp soil. Keep well watered during dry weather. Space plants about 30 cm apart. Fish plant grows happily in a pot and does equally well in tropical and temperate climates although in cold regions the whole plant dies back in winter to reappear in spring. It forms a dense mat and can become invasive.

Garden talk

Fish plant leaves are strongly flavoured, with a unique pungency. In Vietnam and Cambodia, they are wrapped, in varying combinations with other herb and salad plants, in rice paper, dipped in sauces and eaten during the meal. They are a delicious fresh garnish for dishes made from eggs and strongly flavoured meat and fish. Fiona says that the leaves have a strong meaty flavour and she uses them in soup, 'You finely shred them and put them in at the last minute. It is rich in vitamin C.' Ruyet uses leaves in salad and also recommends putting them into a food processor and giving young children a few drops to drink to reduce a temperature. She says it helps alleviate the symptoms of chicken pox too. The Vietnamese also eat it to relieve haemorrhoids and stomach cramps while in China, fish plant is used to treat rashes.

Five-seasons herb

Plectranthus amboinicus

This plant is succulent and softly hairy with a sprawling habit. It grows to 60 cm with thick, scalloped pale green leaves that sometimes have reddish markings. There is a variegated form where the leaves have pale yellow margins. Flowers are pale pink. The whole plant has a strong scent similar to oregano, but with an extra spiciness.

Grow

Grow from seed or cuttings taken in spring. This perennial tropical plant will not survive cold, damp weather but grows easily in the tropics. It is best regarded as an annual in really cold regions. It grows well in a pot, but in cooler regions try moving it inside to a sunny window sill, make sure not to over water, and it may survive through winter. From time to time, nip back new growth to encourage a bushier habit.

Garden talk

Finely chopped leaves are sprinkled into soups, stews, and egg and tomato dishes, and added to strongly flavoured fish and meat dishes, like goat and mutton. The flavour of the

Five-seasons herb

VIETNAMESE RECIPE FROM THIEP

Sour Fish Soup

60 g wet tamarind
1 cup boiling water
1½ litres water
1 tablespoon sugar
½ teaspoon salt
2 teaspoons chicken stock powder
1 whole fish (Bream) approximately 700 g, cleaned and scaled
1 tomato, cut in quarters
200 g taro stems, peeled and sliced
200 g snake beans, cut in half
200 g mung bean sprouts, washed and trimmed
1 hot red chilli, finely sliced
3 tablespoons fish sauce
2 spring onions, finely chopped
2 tablespoons coriander, finely chopped
2 tablespoons five-seasons herb, finely chopped

Soak wet tamarind in 1 cup boiling water for 15 minutes. Mash, sieve and set liquid aside.

Bring water to the boil in a large stock pot. Add sugar, salt and stock powder. Add fish, cover and simmer until cooked (approximately 5 minutes). Do not overcook. Lift out fish, remove cooked flesh from the bones, discard the bones and keep the flesh warm. Add tomato, taro stems, snake beans, bean sprouts and chilli to the stock. Cover and simmer until just cooked. Add 4 tablespoons tamarind water and fish sauce to the stock, and adjust salt and sugar to taste. Bring stock back to the boil, return fish to the pot, and immediately turn off the heat. Cover and let stand for 2 minutes until fish is warmed through. Serve at once into bowls and garnish with spring onions, coriander and five-seasons herb. Makes 4 large serves, or 6 accompanied with steamed rice.

leaves combines particularly well with beans, so try stirring a finely chopped leaf into bean salad or soup. Thiep uses five-seasons herb to treat coughs and generally for the lungs. She says you can add it to soup, or you wash it and put it into a food processor with water and then drink it. She adds that this is her favourite herb, 'I slice this and put it on top of the sour fish soup.'

Garland chrysanthemum

Chrysanthemum coronarium var. *spatiosum*

Garland chrysanthemum

This is an annual that grows initially from a single, tender, round stalk with finely-cut, green leaves. If not harvested, the plants will grow to 1 m and develop daisy-like yellow flowers over a long period. The flowers of the most common form are golden in the centre and pale creamy-yellow on the outside. There are several cultivars that vary in leaf shape and size.

Grow

Grow from seed sown in the garden in early spring or autumn. Thin plants to about 15 cm apart. Garland chrysanthemum grows best in a nutrient and humus-rich soil in full sun. Plants need to be watered regularly. Pick the first leaves about 30 days after sowing.

Leaves are at their best when plants are young, as they become bitter as the plant ages. Remove the flower heads from most of the plants to encourage more leaf growth, but allow a couple to flower so plants will self-sow.

Garden talk

The strongly aromatic leaves and stems are eaten as a vegetable by steaming, blanching or boiling in a tiny amount of water. Serve with a little soy sauce and sesame oil. Don't overcook as this makes them bitter. Fresh young leaves are high in vitamin A and are an interesting ingredient in leafy salads. Mrs Poon says that she mainly eats the leaves in soup and adds that you put them in the hot water and then they are cooked. Tju Ing also adds the young leaves to soup. The Vietnamese use the leaves in chicken, pork and beef dishes and fried as a vegetable.

Garlic

Allium sativum

A whole bed of young garlic plants

Garlic is a flat-leafed perennial that is usually grown as an annual. Plants grow to about 40 cm and in some cultivars, in late summer, a rounded stalk appears from the centre of the plant. This stalk bears a rounded flower head containing a cluster of bulbils and occasional pinkish-white flowers.

Grow

Grow garlic by dividing the familiar bulb and planting the individual cloves from autumn to early spring, or by planting the bulbils found in the flower head of some cultivars. Plant cloves about 2 cm below the surface of the soil and space them 10 cm apart in rows 40 cm apart. Garlic does best in light soils with good drainage, enrich the soil with well-rotted manure before planting, and top dress with blood and bone during winter and early spring. Mulch around the plants and water regularly while the bulbs are growing. Harvest garlic about eight months after planting by digging up the whole plant with a fork and shaking gently to remove excess dirt.

Garden talk

Garlic has numerous culinary and medicinal properties. It is an essential

CHILEAN RECIPE FROM AGUSTIN
GRILLED OR BARBECUED STEAK

1 whole bulb garlic, peeled and crushed
1 teaspoon dried oregano
1 teaspoon ground cumin
½ teaspoon freshly ground black pepper
2 tablespoons olive oil
1 teaspoon salt
1 kg sliced steak

Place all ingredients (except steak) into a mortar and pound to a paste.
   Marinate the steak in this mix for several hours or overnight.
Barbecue or grill until cooked. **Serves 4.**

ingredient in savoury dishes all over the world. The Chinese eat garlic as sprouts, green garlic and garlic cloves. Freshly sprouted garlic leaves are added to salads and stir-fries. Niu Jia says that garlic is a very good medicine, 'In China we have the saying that garlic has 100 advantages, just one disadvantage, not good for eyesight.' He adds that it also helps to promote immunity. Tawfik tells us what to do when the garlic is harvested. 'Hang it in an airy dark place and cut it as you need it. Otherwise it will rot.' He harvested 50 or 60 bulbs from his garden last year.

ETHIOPIAN RECIPE FROM BASRA
Garlic and Chilli Salsa

3 large (or 6 small) cloves garlic, peeled and finely chopped
100 g mixed red chillies, de-seeded and chopped
1 onion, sliced
2 tomatoes, roughly chopped
juice 1 lemon
1 teaspoon salt
½ teaspoon freshly ground black pepper

Blend all ingredients together in a food processor or blender. Serve as an accompaniment to meat dishes. Store any leftover salsa in an airtight jar in the refrigerator.

Garlic chives
Allium tuberosum

Garlic chives are perennials that grow from large spreading rhizomes with green strap-like leaves to a height of 40 cm. The flowers are white, star-like and sweetly scented.

Grow
Propagate from seed sown at any time or by dividing clumps. Plant in clumps of about 10 plants, with 20 cm between clumps. They are not fussy about soil. Garlic chives will grow in most climates,

Garlic chives

CHINESE RECIPE FROM SHU XIAN
Pork Dumplings with Garlic Chives

150 g minced pork
½ cup garlic chives, chopped
⅓ cup fresh water chestnuts, peeled and finely grated or
⅓ cup tinned water chestnuts, drained and finely grated
½ cup Chinese cabbage, finely chopped
¼ cup *pak choi*, finely chopped
4 tablespoons fresh ginger, peeled and grated

2 tablespoons coriander leaves and stems, finely chopped
1 teaspoon salt
½ teaspoon ground pepper
3 teaspoons corn flour
1 egg, lightly beaten
1 packet round wonton skins

Place all ingredients except the wonton skins in a bowl and mix together thoroughly. Place 1 teaspoon of mixture in centre of each wonton skin. Dampen around the edge of each skin with a little water, fold in half to form a semicircle and press edges together firmly to seal. These dumplings can then be simmered in soups, steamed or deep fried until golden brown. Mixture makes 64 dumplings producing leafy growth for most of the year and flowers in summer. In warmer areas they do not die back and may self-sow prolifically, so remove the flower heads before they set seed. Leaves are harvested by cutting them just below the soil surface, as much of the flavour is in the base of the leaf. To harvest flower buds, cut at the base of the stem before the bud opens.

Garden talk

Leaves, flower stems and flowers are all eaten and have a distinct garlic-onion flavour. They are high in vitamins A and C as well as iron and calcium. The leaves are often added to noodle dishes or used with bean curd, spring rolls and omelettes. They are also dressed with salt and sesame oil and served as a salad. Amy and Chitzu grow garlic chives and use them to fill dumplings, and stir-fried with eggs, or with bean sprouts. They also say that the whole stalk with the bud is very tasty and add that garlic chives are good for health too. 'They are similar to garlic and will kill bacteria in the intestine.' Niu Jia points out that you only use the leaves, not the bulb. The leaves are ground and the juice drunk to ease bronchial problems, and a paste made from the leaves and roots is used to ease the pain from toothache.

Gotu kola

Centella asiatica

Gotu kola

This creeping perennial plant is also known as Indian pennywort and grows to only 20 cm. It puts out slender stolons with distinct nodes. Roots and clumps of round, heart-shaped, crinkled leaves grow from these nodes as the plant spreads over the ground. The flowers are red or purple-red in colour.

Grow

Grow from seed sown in spring, or by division in spring or autumn. Place plants about 30 cm apart. This herb does best in moist ground but will also tolerate dry periods. It is not fussy about soil and will do well in sun or semi-shade. In cooler regions, gotu kola is dormant in winter with little or no growth, and it may even die back. In spring it will start to grow rapidly again, and under ideal conditions may become a pest.

Garden talk

Gotu kola is commonly used as a vegetable and a medicine. Leaves are eaten raw as part of a salad. They are also steamed and added to rice or used as a garnish on soups and stews. Thai says that she eats this plant raw or if she has plenty of leaves she puts them with a little water and sugar into a food processor and drinks the resulting liquid. She believes it will bring down a temperature. Gotu kola is useful in improving blood circulation, reducing inflammation in arthritis, stimulating hair and nail growth and helping to cure skin diseases. This herb should not be eaten regularly by anyone with high blood pressure or anyone who takes blood-thinning drugs.

Greater celandine
Chelidonium majus

Greater celandine is a perennial with blue-green leaves and clear golden-yellow flowers. The whole plant grows to about 90 cm. The leaves and stems contain a bright orange juice that is poisonous and can be irritating to the skin.

Grow

Grow greater celandine from seeds sown in spring, or by root division in autumn. It prefers a semi-shaded position but is not fussy about soil and will self-sow readily around the garden.

Garden talk

While this plant has medicinal uses it should not be taken internally without medical supervision as it can be poisonous in large doses. Ida calls this plant milkweed and says it is a skin doctor. 'If you have a wart the sap actually doesn't make any harm but the wart stops growing and after a while it disappears.' She adds that in Russia now it is used to treat some stomach complaints but emphasises that it needs to be done very carefully.

Greater celandine

Horehound

Horehound
Marrubium vulgare

Horehound is a perennial that grows as a small shrub to 60 cm. The leaves are pale green, opposite, rounded, and wrinkled in texture. Stems and undersides of the leaves are softly hairy and white. Tiny two-lipped flowers are white and occur at the top of the plant.

Grow

Horehound is a declared noxious weed in some places and really should not be planted in a garden as it so readily colonises waste places, particularly rocky areas and roadsides. It can be grown though from seed sown in spring or summer into any reasonable soil or it can be harvested from the wild.

Julia calls this plant *toronjil cuyano* and uses it medicinally. A tea made from the fresh or dried leaves is drunk to treat cold and flu symptoms, especially coughs. Take three to four times a day, hot or cold; add honey to improve the flavour as it is very bitter.

Leeks

Allium ampeloprasum
Porrum Group

Leeks are biennials that grow from strong root systems, with flat, broad, linear leaves that are folded lengthwise. The elongated foliage leaf-bases encircle each other to form a cylindrical elongated stem and bulb. Solid flower stems can reach a height of 1.5 metres and are topped by big, round flower heads made up of hundreds of pink or white flowers.

Leeks

Grow
Leeks are usually grown from seed, which can be sown in autumn, spring or summer, depending on the climate and the cultivar grown. They need a long growing season and in cold climates should be planted as early in spring as possible. Sow into seed trays or directly into the soil. Transplant into trenches or into individual holes when seedlings reach 20 centimetres. Average spacing is 15 centimetres apart in rows or up to 30 centimetres apart in a block. Leeks are generally easy to grow, but do best in a rich, well-drained soil in an open position with plenty of moisture during the growing season.

Garden talk
Leek stalks have a mellow flavour, reminiscent of onion and garlic but sweeter and milder. High in vitamins A, C and E, leeks are also a good source of iron and fibre. Young, tender leeks are added raw to salads. They are also steamed, boiled, fried and added to soups, casseroles and stir-fries. Sophie grows leeks and loves to cook them with rice. 'We chop the leeks into small parts, the centre, chop them, chop them, then we put the onion and garlic and leeks and tomato in with the rice, leave the rice to boil and leave with a little bit of water. After you cook it add a little lemon. It's delicious.'

Lemon balm

Lemon balm

Melissa officinalis

Lemon balm is a mint-like plant that grows as a bush to about 60 cm. It has a square branching stem and oval toothed leaves with a fragrant lemon odour and taste. The small white flowers bloom right through summer.

Grow

Grow lemon balm from seed sown in spring or autumn, by dividing clumps of roots in early spring, or by cuttings taken from new growth in spring. It is shallow-rooted, so needs plenty of water during hot weather. Cut back after flowering. Lemon balm grows well in most soils as long as they are well drained. It self-sows readily so can become weedy in some gardens.

Garden talk

Lemon balm's delicious lemon fragrance combines well with fish and chicken, as well as fruit dishes. It makes a delightful lemon tea, which will help to ease anxiety and headaches and lift the mood. Vilma calls lemon balm *toronjil* and drinks tea made from its leaves when she feels tired. Fresh leaves rubbed onto bites and stings relieve pain and swelling.

Lemon grass
Cymbopogon citratus

The lemony leaves of lemon grass are typically grass-like, growing up to 1 m from bulbous stolons with arching leaf blades. The plant rarely flowers. Clumps often grow to 1 m across.

Grow

Lemon grass needs a sheltered, warm, sunny position, with plenty of water in summer. A bad frost will severely retard or kill it, and wet, cold winters will make it look brown and straggly. Mulch well during hot summers and feed with rotted manure in early spring. It likes a nutrient-rich, well-drained soil and full sun. Propagate new plants by dividing clumps, and space plants at least 50 cm apart. Lemon grass grows well in a large pot.

Garden talk

The distinctive lemon fragrance of lemon grass is essential to many dishes. Harvest outside stems that are at least 1 cm across. If using it whole, just cut off the top leafy portion, bruise the base and add to the dish. Remove before serving. To slice or mince, use the bottom 15 cm or so of the stems, peeling away the outer layers until a pinkish-white colour appears. The tender centre is then finely sliced or minced. Fiona stirs finely chopped leaves and stems into chicken curries and Mor adds stem bases to chicken soup. Minced stems are added to stuffing for fish and chicken, or stirred into a marinade. Fresh or dried leaves make a delicious lemon flavoured tea. Jesus drinks the tea when she has a cold while Tai uses lemon grass leaves combined with lemon leaves, puts them in a pot and boils them. 'If you've got flu you put a blanket over you and slowly breathe the steam and feel better.'

Lemon grass growing next to edible canna.

VIETNAMESE RECIPE FROM TAI
Stir-Fried Chicken with Lemon Grass and Chilli

3 tablespoons vegetable oil
1 large onion, sliced
1½ cm piece fresh ginger, peeled and grated
2 cloves garlic, chopped
3 stalks lemon grass, finely chopped (pinkish-white part only)
3 long red chillies, finely chopped
1½ kg chicken drumettes
1 teaspoon salt
1 tablespoon sugar
2 tablespoons fish sauce
½ cup chicken stock
coriander and Vietnamese mint leaves, finely chopped

Heat oil in a large non-stick wok or frying pan, and stir-fry onion, ginger and garlic until translucent. Add lemon grass and chillies and stir-fry 2 minutes. Add chicken pieces and stir-fry until browned. Sprinkle the salt and sugar over the chicken and cook, stirring, until sugar has melted and slightly caramelised. Add fish sauce and stock, and cook gently until chicken is tender (approximately 45 minutes).

Serve garnished with coriander and Vietnamese mint. **Serves 4.**

Lemon verbena
Aloysia triphylla

Lemon verbena is a deciduous perennial shrub or small tree that can grow up to 5 m. It has narrow, pointed pale green leaves with a strong lemony scent and flavour and light mauve to white flowers.

Grow
Grow from tip cuttings taken from the new growth in spring. Bushes need to be pruned back by two-thirds at the beginning of spring, and can be cut and used progressively during summer. They are extremely fast growing. Lemon verbena likes a sunny, open position and will grow in any reasonable well-drained soil.

Garden talk
Leaves are used for tea, added to chicken or fish, or dried for potpourri and scented sachets. Agustin adds a lemon verbena leaf to his cup of tea and Vilma says that it is a good medicine. She adds, 'In my country when somebody had died they would cut it and put it inside the house to get rid of any illnesses or viruses that were brought from the cemetery. The lemon leaves: they used to burn these leaves to get rid of the germs, this is used as a disinfectant.'

Lemon verbena

Lettuce

Lactuca sativa

and Stem lettuce

L. sativa var. *asparagina*

Rows of assorted leafy lettuces

Stem lettuce.

Many types of lettuce are grown in the gardens. These are mostly leafy lettuces like oakleaf, cos and butter forms, and the very different stem lettuce. The gardeners refer to a lot of leafy plants as 'lettuce' because they are used in salads. These include leafy cabbage plants, endive and even watercress. Stem lettuce, as indicated by its name, is grown for its elongated stem. It starts as a typical lettuce with a loose cluster of light green leaves. From this grows a central stalk with smaller leaves at the top. This stem elongates and can reach more than 1 m in height, but it is usually harvested before this.

Grow

All lettuces are grown in a range of climates. They will tolerate mild frosts, but seed will not germinate in very hot weather. In temperate regions, grow them from seed sown in autumn, winter or spring. Space plants about 30 cm apart. Lettuce likes full sun, a fertile soil that is well drained and regular water. Harvest leaves whenever they are needed. Harvest stem lettuce when it is 30–40 cm long and at least 2 cm across. Cut a few centimetres above the ground.

Garden talk

Leafy lettuces are used in all sorts of salads as well as being added to stir-fries and some other cooked dishes. Peel stem lettuce stems before use as the outer layer contains a bitter sap. Once this layer is removed only the pale green, soft core is left. This is diced or sliced and eaten fresh or cooked by boiling, braising, stir-frying

or stewing. The stem has a subtle, cucumber-lettuce flavour and a crisp texture, and is regarded as a delicacy by many Asian people. Georgia grows and uses lettuce all the time and she says that in Greece you can't grow lettuce in the summer because it is too hot. Amy and Chitzu have experimented with growing oakleaf lettuce amongst their more traditional vegetables.

Long-leafed coriander

Eryngium foetidum

Long-leafed coriander

This plant, also known as culantro, is a low-growing herb to about 40 cm that grows as a rosette of stiff, dark green, toothed leaves. Strong stalks grow from the centre and these are topped by pale green, tiny, pineapple-shaped flower heads. The whole plant is strongly pungent with a scent and flavour resembling coriander.

Grow

Long-leafed coriander is a short-lived perennial that is treated as an annual in temperate regions. Grow from seed, which can take several weeks to germinate, sown in seed trays in winter or early spring. Plant seedlings once they are big enough to handle. Space plants about 30 cm apart in all directions. It grows in most soils as long as they are well drained, and likes a position in semi shade or with morning sun, as very hot afternoon sun causes it to wilt. Remove the flower heads to

---

HMONG RECIPE FROM CHUE

UA LAJ (BEEF WITH HERBS)

¼ cup uncooked glutinous or sticky rice grain
1 kg minced beef
1 teaspoon salt
1 bunch long-leafed coriander, chopped
4 spring onions, chopped
¼ bunch coriander leaves and stems, chopped
1 stalk lemon grass, finely chopped (pinkish white part only)
5 hot red chillies, finely chopped (no seeds)
leaves of 2 stems of Vietnamese mint, chopped
½ bunch mint leaves, chopped
juice 3 large lemons
1 tablespoon fish sauce

In a non-stick frying pan, dry fry the rice until golden brown, stirring. Grind to a fine powder using a mortar and pestle. Set aside. Add minced beef and salt to the frying pan and fry in its own fat, stirring, until browned. Drain off the liquid and reserve. Add the herbs and lemon juice to the meat and cook for a further few minutes. Stir in the rice flour, fish sauce and meat juice and heat through.

Place in a serving dish and serve cold with lettuce leaves and cooked sticky rice. **Serves 4.**

encourage leaf growth, and water once a month or so with liquid seaweed fertiliser or fish emulsion.

Garden talk

Leaves are eaten fresh and cooked in a range of dishes, especially those where the flavour of another ingredient needs to be disguised. Finely chopped leaves make an excellent garnish on all sorts of dishes, but fish dishes in particular.

Stir chopped leaves into soups; add to steamed rice or toss into mixed vegetables, curries and curry pastes. Mien says that this herb is very hard to obtain and this makes it very expensive. She adds that in a restaurant you are only given one leaf on top of a beef dish because it is so expensive. Thiep likes to serve it with beef or chicken soup, just chopped and put on top.

Luffa

Luffa spp.

Angled luffa (*L. acutangula*) and smooth luffa (*L. cylindrica*) are vigorous vines with hairy stems and branching tendrils. The large, rough, lobed leaves are oval, while the male and female flowers are yellow, with female flowers occurring singly and male flowers in groups. Angled luffa fruits are elongated and cylindrical in shape, with ten strong ribs. Smooth luffa fruits have no ribs and are usually larger, but are otherwise similar to angled luffa.

Luffas

Grow

Grow from seeds sown in spring and summer, where they are to grow, about 50 cm apart. Soak seeds in water for 24 hours before planting. Plants grow best when trained up a trellis about 2 m high. They are frost-sensitive and cold weather may cause young fruit to drop off the plant. Luffas do best in well-drained, sandy soils that are rich in organic matter. Water regularly during dry weather. Begin harvesting fruit once they are 10 cm long. If the fruits are allowed to get too big they become fibrous and start to produce chemicals that can cause diarrhoea.

Garden talk

Luffas are grown by only a few Chinese gardeners in the gardens. To prepare the fruit, they wash them well and use a peeler or sharp knife to take the sharp edges off the ridges. Young luffas are sliced and eaten raw in salads, or cooked as a vegetable by boiling, frying, steaming or braising. They are also added to soups and stir-fries with other vegetables. Their mild, slightly bitter flavour combines well with fresh herbs, with coconut milk, and in particular with vegetable curries. Young leaves and flower buds are also eaten cooked as a vegetable on their own, or combined with other vegetables in a stir-fry. Smooth luffa fruits can be picked and eaten when young but they are usually left to fully mature which takes four to five months from planting. The fruit are then treated and the internal skeleton used as a sponge.

Malabar spinach
Basella alba

There are two main varieties of Malabar spinach, one with fleshy green stems and leaves and white flowers (B. *alba*), the other with red-purple stems and purple-green leaves with pink flowers (B. *alba* 'Rubra'). They are both short-lived perennials with large oval leaves and a twisting climbing growth habit.

Grow
Grow from cuttings or seed. Seed will germinate more readily if they are soaked in water first and if the soil is over 18°C. In temperate regions, start seed inside in individual pots and transplant outside when the last chance of frost is over because plants are very frost-tender. In warmer regions, plant directly into soil that has been enriched with plenty of manure. Plant at the base of a trellis or tripod or in a hanging basket. Malabar spinach will not grow vigorously until the weather really warms up. In regions with very hot, dry summers, it will need plenty of water and may need to be shaded during hot afternoons.

Garden talk
Stems, young shoots and leaves are all eaten. They are high in vitamins A and C and a good source of iron and calcium. Fresh leaves are added to salads and they make a good substitute for spinach in any recipe, retaining their bright green colour. The red form turns green when cooked. Malabar spinach is delicious in stir-fries as long as it is not overcooked as it will then become slimy and mucilaginous, giving rise to its other name of slippery vegetable. Leaves are also added to soups and stews where the mucilaginous qualities can be used for thickening. A delicious soup, known in China as slippery soup, can be made by adding Malabar spinach, water, bean curd and hard-boiled eggs to freshly fried ginger. Mien calls this plant *rau mung toi* and says that the Australian form has a larger leaf than the one they grew in Vietnam, and Tju Ing likes to cook it with garlic and oil

Malabar spinach

Mallow

Malva spp.

Mallows are common weeds in Australia with three species being the most commonly found: Dwarf mallow (M. *neglecta*), small-flowered mallow (M. *parviflora*) and tall mallow (M. *sylvestris*). The tallest grow to well over 1 m. All these mallows have rounded leaves with scalloped margins and pink, purple or white flowers. The flowers are followed by button-like seedpods.

Grow

New plants grow easily from seed, but they appear so readily in the average garden that it is probably not necessary to actually plant them. They will grow in any soil in almost any position.

Garden talk

Mallows are used in medicine for the mucilage in their leaves, mainly as a cough remedy. Leaves, young shoots and immature seedpods are all edible either fresh in salads or cooked. Kerama calls mallow *khobaza* and says that it is frequently used in Egypt. 'We use the leaves in soup. They are good for the blood.' Fiona maintains that it is really a nice vegetable. 'Cut it off close to the ground, wash it very carefully and pull off the dead leaves. I just leave it whole and put it in a big pot with oil, garlic and chilli sauce and a little bit of water. I cook it until it goes down and is a bit limp, then a little bit longer to soften it up; it is very soft and tender and succulent. To eat it you strip off the leaves and chomp, chomp, chomp down to the tender bit and then throw away the stalk. It is fun to eat. I use a sweet chilli sauce.'

Mallow

EGYPTIAN RECIPE FROM KERAMA

KHOBAZA SOUP

150 g mallow leaves
3½ cups chicken stock
2 tablespoons rice
1 tablespoon butter
3 cloves garlic, crushed
1 teaspoon freshly ground coriander seed

Pick mallow leaves from stems, weigh and wash well. Place in a saucepan, cover with hot water, bring to the boil then simmer, covered, for 10 minutes. Drain, and blend in a food processor or blender. In a saucepan, heat chicken stock and add blended mallow leaves and rice. Cover and simmer until rice is nearly cooked.

Meanwhile, melt butter in a saucepan and add garlic and coriander seeds. Gently fry a few minutes until fragrant then add to the soup. Bring soup back to a simmer for 5 minutes, then serve. **Serves 4.**

Marigold
Calendula officinalis

Marigold is a hardy annual herb that grows to a height of about 50 cm with soft green leaves and single or double flowers that range from yellow through to orange with tints of red.

Grow

Grow marigolds from seed sown in spring and summer. They grow in most soils as long as they are well drained. Regular tip pruning (or keep picking the flowers) helps to keep them flowering and stops plants from becoming straggly. Harvest flowers and leaves at any time. Dry the petals by pulling them from the flower heads and spreading on sheets of newspaper. They are dry when they feel like tissue paper.

Garden talk

Add fresh marigold petals and leaves to salads and sandwiches and stir the petals, fresh or dried through cooked rice. Lioudmila uses marigolds all the time. 'Every day the leaves go in the salad and the flowers go for tea. It is very good for the hormonal system.' Fresh petals are also rubbed into bites and stings to relieve pain and swelling. Oscar grows a lot of marigolds and says they are the best things for the lymph system and he also rubs the petals onto the skin for bruises and scratches. 'It is antiseptic and will fight off infection.' Adelina says, 'I feel sorry cutting the marigolds sometimes but I say please forgive me that I take you, you are used for healing. It makes me feel very happy.' She dries the flowers first, just on a tray in the house and puts two or three flowers into a cup to make tea. 'The perfume is incredible. There is no harm to it and it actually cleanses the blood.' She adds that she believes it is also an anti-cancer plant.

Marigold

RUSSIAN RECIPE FROM ADELINA
RAW VEGETABLE SALAD

All the vegetables should be in roughly equal quantities.
½ small beetroot, peeled and grated
½ medium carrot, grated
1 Lebanese cucumber, grated
1 wedge cabbage, finely chopped
½ red onion, finely chopped
½ Granny Smith apple, grated with skin on
chives, coriander, parsley, dill, marigold leaves (the more the better), finely chopped
light sour cream

Toss all ingredients into a salad bowl. Add just enough light sour cream to moisten the salad. Add salt and pepper to taste. Toss well and serve. **Serves 2.**

RUSSIAN RECIPE FROM LIOUDMILA
MARIGOLD TINCTURE

12 dried marigold flowers
100 mL alcohol (vodka or brandy can be used)

Combine the flowers and alcohol. Leave to stand for a week, shaking occasionally. Use a few drops of the tincture on cotton wool as a disinfectant and to enhance wound healing.

Melons

Benincasa spp.

Both winter melons (*B. hispida*) and fuzzy melons (*B. hispida* var. *chieh-gua*) are very vigorous climbing annuals with coarse, hairy stems and trailing tendrils. They have very large, lobed, dark green leaves and bright yellow flowers. Winter melon fruit (also known as wax gourds) are more rounded than oblong, may be hairy when young but the hairs disappear when mature and a waxy bloom covers the surface of the melon. Fuzzy melon fruit are generally plump and elongated, longer than wide and covered in fine hairs.

Grow

Both melons need a long, warm growing season, often more than five months, to reach maturity. Plant into well-drained soil that has been well manured and make sure there is plenty of space. Winter melons are best grown on the ground so that the fruits can be allowed to grow to their full size without support while fuzzy melons do well on trellises. Germinate seed on wet paper, using a heated propagator with bottom heat of about 28°C. Seed should sprout in three to five days. Plant into individual pots and transplant into the garden once the seedlings are about 18 cm tall. If planting directly into the soil, place four or five seeds in each position and thin to the healthiest plant once they are growing vigorously. Nip out the growing tips after about three weeks, to leave four lateral shoots. Begin picking young winter melons when they are three to four weeks old, the optimum size then is about 1.5 kg. They can reach 20 kg, but once they are as big as this they are only useful in soups or stews. Pick young fuzzy melons when they are three to four weeks old, about 12 cm long and still covered by fine hairs.

Fuzzy melon

CHINESE RECIPE FROM AMY
Winter Melon Soup

2 chicken marylands, halved
325 g smoked pork, diced
8 cups water
2 tablespoons dried shrimp
2 tablespoons red bean paste
500 g winter melon

Put the chicken pieces, smoked pork and water into a large stockpot. Bring to the boil, cover and simmer 1 hour. Add dried shrimp and red bean paste and simmer a further 30 minutes. Peel the melon, scrape out the seeds and cut into 2 cm pieces. Add to the soup and continue to simmer for a further 30 minutes. Place a piece of chicken in each bowl and pour the soup over the top. **Serves 4.**

Garden talk

Young melons are eaten as a vegetable, cooked in the same way as marrows and zucchini. Winter melons taste like a slightly sweet zucchini, while fuzzy melons have a slightly stronger more distinctive flavour. Fuzzy melons are particularly good stuffed. Before cutting fuzzy melons, always remove the fine hairs on the outside by rubbing with paper and then washing in cold water. The leaves, young growing tips, flower buds and seeds are also eaten. Flower buds and growing tips are cooked as a vegetable, added to stir-fries or chopped and sprinkled over a salad. Amy and Chitzu use winter melons in soup and say that in China they are regarded as a very good medicine. 'In hot weather you can eat it to reduce heat and cool your body.' They add that the soup is helpful for anyone recovering from illness.

Mint

Mentha spp.

Spearmint

The mint family is extremely varied and it is often difficult to identify individual species because of their tendency to hybridise. Mints most commonly used in the gardens have a definite spearmint or peppermint flavour, and so are probably varieties of M. *piperita*, peppermint, and M. *spicata*, spearmint. Mints generally grow to about 60 cm with long, green rounded or lance-shaped leaves. Flowers are pink or mauve. All mints spread by underground runners.

Grow

Mints can be grown from seed, by taking cuttings or by dividing clumps. Take cuttings of non-flowering growth in spring or summer; divide plants at any time. Any piece that has some root growth will produce a new plant. Mints will grow in most soils as long as they are not too dry; they even tolerate heavy clay. They grow in sun or semi-shade. Most mints spread aggressively, so plant into a container or into an individual bed to stop them taking over the garden.

Garden talk

Mints are probably the most universally grown herb in the gardens with all cultures using it in food and/or for medicine. Mint is also added to salads and is an essential ingredient in a range of culturally significant dishes. It is also used medicinally especially for indigestion. Alonzo says that *yerbowena*, the Spanish name for mint, means 'the good weed'. Jesus puts mint into chicken soup and says that it is good for the stomach, while Julia grows three different types of mint and also uses them for stomach-aches. Vilma adds mint to almost every meal while

EL SALVADOREAN RECIPE FROM VILMA
GIRELLO

Part one
1 kg girello meat in the piece
1 carrot, thickly sliced
2 potatoes, diced
1 onion, roughly chopped
1 clove garlic, finely chopped
2 tablespoons chicken stock powder
2 bay leaves
1 tablespoon dried oregano
1 teaspoon salt

Part two
½ onion, finely chopped
½ green capsicum finely chopped
2–3 radishes, finely chopped
½ bunch mint leaves, finely chopped
1–2 tomatoes, finely chopped
1 lemon, flesh only, finely chopped

Part three
8 whole black peppercorns
4 cloves garlic
1 onion, finely chopped
6 bay leaves
6 cloves
1 teaspoon dried oregano
1½ teaspoons ground cumin
1 teaspoon salt

Place all ingredients from part one in a large soup pot, cover with water, bring to the boil, cover and simmer until meat is cooked and tender – approximately 3½ hours. Remove the cooked meat, the remaining soup can then be used as a separate meal by adding a few more ingredients.

Mince the meat or chop finely, place in a large bowl and add all ingredients from part two, mix well.

Place all ingredients from part three into a mortar and pound to a rough paste. In a large saucepan, heat the pounded spices until fragrant. Add the meat mix, cover and heat until warmed through. Serve with cooked rice or beans. **Serves 4.**

Marcos likes it with cooked food but not in salads or for tea. Ida drinks mint tea and says, 'It stops cramps, so if you have a glass of tea with mint you will have a good sleep.' Rawda describes how she makes mint tea: 'Put the water in the pot and put it on the heat until it boils and then put the tea inside and after it has boiled take it off and put the mint in. We add sugar as required. We drink it hot. We drink it all day. If we are alone we drink it, if we have any visitors we drink it. The whole day we drink tea with mint.' Aesha also has tea with mint but says it has the best smell and taste in summer and Kerama says that mint tea is a beautiful relaxant. Edite uses mint tea to help with blocked noses and ease breathing, she also adds mint to salads and stir-fries and will put some in the water when she is cooking fish. Maria adds mint to stuffed tomatoes and Sophie puts it in dolmades and stuffed peppers as well. Mai, Chue and Mor mix mint with mince and serve it with rice noodles; they'll also add a sprig of mint to soup just before they serve it.

Molokhia
Corchorus olitorius

This annual plant is also known as Devil's mallow, Jew's mallow and Turkish spinach and is a native of North Africa. It grows as a bush to about 50 cm with oval to lance-shaped green leaves.

Grow

Grow molokhia from seed sown in spring into good humus-rich soil in full sun. Plants grow well in hot, dry regions where it has weed potential if the water supply is good. Leaves are harvested right through the growing season from late spring to autumn.

Garden talk

Leaves are high in Vitamins A and C, calcium, iron and magnesium. When cooked they develop a mucilaginous consistency, like mallow and okra, that can be something of an acquired taste. Leaves are added to soups and stews or eaten on their own like spinach. Ibrahim grows a lot of molokhia. He says the best time to harvest it is in summer because it doesn't grow in winter. He collects his own seeds in autumn to sow them again the following spring. 'We chop it and then we cook it. When it is boiled properly you put the garlic and meat stock together in order for it to be cooked.' Aesha chops molokhia and cooks it with onion, oil, spices, tomato, meat and hot pepper. She says you can substitute *regla* (purslane) in the same recipe. 'If we have the molokhia we put molokhia, if we have *regla* we put *regla*.' Rawda uses fennel to add flavour to her molokhia while Kerama adds molokhia to chicken broth.

Molokhia

EGYPTIAN RECIPE FROM KERAMA
EGYPTIAN GREENS SOUP

6 cups chicken stock
1 kg chicken fillets, diced
400 g fresh (or 1 packet of frozen) molokhia leaves
1 tablespoon tomato paste
1 hot chilli, finely chopped
1 bay leaf
1 onion, finely chopped
½ teaspoon ground cardamom
1 teaspoon freshly ground black pepper
10 cloves garlic
2 tablespoons ground coriander
1 teaspoon salt
2 tablespoons butter or margarine
juice of 1 lemon
1 teaspoon Tabasco sauce or ½ teaspoon cayenne pepper
½ bunch fresh coriander, finely chopped

In a large soup pot, bring chicken stock to the boil and add diced chicken fillets. Lower heat and simmer, covered, for 5 minutes. If using fresh molokhia leaves, wash them and chop finely. Add the fresh (or frozen, thawed) leaves. Add tomato paste, chilli, bay leaf, onion, cardamom and black pepper. Cover and simmer for 20 minutes.

Pound the garlic, ground coriander and salt together in a mortar. Heat the butter in a small saucepan and gently fry the garlic and coriander paste, stirring, until fragrant and slightly browned. Add the garlic mixture and butter to the soup and stir well. Add the lemon juice and Tabasco or cayenne, and simmer gently for a further 5 minutes. This can be garnished with coriander and eaten as it is, or it is often served over hot boiled rice. **Serves 4–6.**

Mugwort

Artemisia vulgaris

Mugwort

A sprawling, vigorous plant, mugwort has dark green leaves with a soft grey downy underside. It can reach to well over 1 m in height when the tiny yellowish flowers are borne on long sprays.

Grow

This plant self-sows readily and, being so vigorous, should be cut back before seeds form because it will take over the garden in some climates. Well-drained sandy loam soils are ideal but mugwort will grow in most conditions and does well beside the sea. Grown from seed or by division in spring, mugwort needs little attention once established, apart from a heavy pruning in autumn.

Garden talk

Mugwort leaves are used in small amounts in both medicine and cooking, but should not be taken internally by pregnant women or any one with intestinal inflammation.

Tai calls mugwort *ngai cuu* and uses it to treat arthritis. When his feet get swollen and sore he heats up a brick, puts some salt on top and then puts *ngai cuu* on top.

'Put your foot on top of the brick and leave it there for an hour and then you will feel better.' He also drinks chicken soup made with *ngai cuu*, to treat his arthritis and says that it is good for head colds and to invigorate blood circulation. Mai, Chue and Mor add mugwort to their chicken soup given to women after childbirth.

VIETNAMESE RECIPE FROM TAI

Black Chicken Soup

1 black chicken (Silky Bantam)
4–6 sprigs mugwort
2 tablespoons sesame seed oil
4 slices ginger, peeled
200 g black beans
8 cups water
1 teaspoon salt
2 cups Chinese rice wine
2 large leaves perilla per person, finely chopped
1 spring onion per person, finely chopped
4 tablespoons cooked rice per person
1 egg yolk per person

Place mugwort sprigs inside chicken.

Heat oil in a frying pan and stir-fry ginger and black beans until fragrant (approximately 2 minutes). Add chicken and fry on all sides until browned.

Transfer chicken, ginger, black beans and oil to a stockpot, add water, salt and Chinese rice wine, and bring to the boil. Cover, lower heat, and simmer gently for 3 hours. In each soup bowl, add perilla, spring onion, rice and egg yolk. Pour boiling soup into each bowl and mix well. Pull some pieces of meat from the chicken, add to each bowl and serve immediately. **Serves 6.**

Nettle

Urtica dioica

Stinging nettles grow to 1 m with dark green, crinkled toothed leaves and small green flowers. The whole plant is downy in appearance and covered with stinging spines, which can be very painful when brushed against. The antidote for the sting is the juice of the stem of the nettle itself, or juice from a dock plant.

Grow

Nettles will grow in almost any soil and under most conditions, but the young shoots growing in rich soil are the tastiest and most nutritious. Grow from seed sown in spring or dig up young plants and transplant into your garden.

Garden talk

Nettles contain iron, calcium, magnesium, potassium, sodium and vitamins A and C. Pick and use only very young leaves and plants that have not started to go to seed. They are at their best in

Nettle

TURKISH RECIPE FROM ZEYNEB

SCRAMBLED EGGS WITH NETTLE

2 tablespoons butter or margarine
⅓ cup lean ham, finely chopped
2 spring onions, finely chopped
⅓ cup young nettle leaves, finely chopped
2 eggs
slice of toast

In a small saucepan, melt butter or margarine. Add ham and spring onions and cook gently, stirring, for approximately 2–3 minutes. Add nettle leaves and stir briefly, then add eggs and continue to cook, stirring constantly, until cooked through but not too dry. Serve immediately on top of toast. **Serves 1.**

TURKISH RECIPE FROM ZEYNEB

NETTLE SOUP

2½ cups chicken stock
1 large clove garlic, crushed
1 hot chilli, seeded and finely chopped
1 cup young nettle leaves, finely chopped
500 g potato, peeled and diced
1 tablespoon cornflour
sour cream, optional

Simmer stock, garlic, chilli, nettles and potato gently in a covered saucepan for 10 minutes until potato is tender. Allow to cool slightly, then puree. In a cup, mix the cornflour with some of the cooled liquid to form a smooth paste. Add this to the soup and heat gently, stirring, until soup has thickened. Serve immediately with a dollop of sour cream if desired. **Serves 4.**

spring as cold weather makes them bitter. When using in a salad, briefly blanch with boiling water and pat dry. Ida says that nettles are good for the soil as well as for people. She adds young nettles to borscht and washes her hair with them. Leaves and young shoots are added to other soups and stews. Both drying and heat dissipates nettle poison so the leaves won't sting. Zeyneb also eats nettles in soup and with scrambled eggs. 'The younger the better. I pick it with a glove and cut it with the scissors.' Georgia adds them to vegetable pie and drinks the water left from boiling them, to clean the blood. Maria uses nettles when making salad, also with vegetable balls and says that they are good for the whole system. 'If you have any condition, nettles will help it.' Vicki makes a salve for arthritis that combines nettles, methylated spirits and aspirin.

Nightshade

Solanum nigrum

Nightshade

This plant is also known as black nightshade and is sometimes mistakenly called belladonna. It should not be confused with the very different poisonous plant *Atropa belladonna* known as deadly nightshade. Nightshade is an annual that grows as a small bush, with woody stems and soft dark-green oval leaves. Drooping, white, star-like flowers are followed by green berries, that turn black or purple when ripe.

Grow
Nightshade grows easily from seed in any soil in almost any position. It will self-sow readily around the garden.

Garden talk
Both young shoots and leaves are eaten as a vegetable or added to soup. Ripe berries are stewed and made into preserves and relishes. Unripe (green) berries should not be eaten. Mrs Poon calls nightshade '*liao* vegies', and says that they are good for diabetes. She adds the leaves and ripe berries to soup. Ana says that it is good for high blood pressure and for diabetes. 'You can cook it with corn and chicken, cook it like spinach. It is a little bit bitter.' She says that in tetum (the language spoken in East Timor) they call it black vegetable. Mai , Chue and Mor say that nightshade is a traditional Hmong vegetable and they stir-fry it by itself as well as adding it to soup.

Okra

Abelmoschus esculentus

Okra in flower

Okra is an annual that grows as a shrub to about 2 m. The whole plant is covered in fine hairs, the stems are woody and the leaves three to five lobed. Flowers are sulphur-yellow with a deep red eye. The dark green fruit are elongated, ridged, pointed at one end and 10–20 cm long. The fruit is very mucilaginous and contains many round dark green, brown, black or white seeds. There are now several cultivars available that vary in height, fruit and flower colour, and cold tolerance.

Grow

Okra does best in direct sunlight and grows in most soils as long as they are well drained and have been prepared with generous additions of organic matter. Plant after the last chance of frost is over. Okra grows easily from seed, as long as soil temperatures are over 15°C, and seed germinates more readily if it has been soaked for twelve hours first. Place seeds about 2 cm deep and 30–40 cm apart. Water regularly during dry weather and mulch around plants to preserve moisture. Wear gloves when picking, as spines on the fruit can irritate the skin of some people. Washing removes the irritating spines, or grow a spineless cultivar like 'Clemsons Spineless' which does well in cooler climates.

EGYPTIAN RECIPE FROM KERAMA

LAMB AND OKRA CASSEROLE

5 large tomatoes
750 g fresh okra, topped and tailed
2 tablespoons oil
3 onions, finely chopped
4 cloves garlic, finely chopped
1 kg lamb, cubed
4 teaspoons salt
2 teaspoons freshly ground black pepper
1 large potato, peeled and diced
2 tablespoons tomato paste
200 mL water
½ bunch coriander, finely chopped
2 lemons, cut into wedges

Place the whole tomatoes in a bowl and pour boiling water over them. Let stand for one minute, then drain, peel and dice. Cut each okra into three. Heat oil in a large saucepan, add onions and garlic, and fry gently until soft. Add lamb, salt and pepper, and brown meat on all sides. Add okra and cook, stirring, until soft. Add tomatoes, potato, tomato paste and water, stir well, and simmer slowly, covered, until meat and vegetables are tender. Serve garnished with coriander, and some lemon wedges for guests to season to their own taste. **Serves 4–6.**

Garden talk

Immature fresh green fruits of okra are steamed, blanched or stir-fried and eaten as a vegetable. Rawda calls them *bamia* and eats them flavoured with *shamar* (fennel) while Kerama says okra are beautiful and loves to cook them with lamb. Okra have a mild oyster flavour but can be something of an acquired taste because of the mucilage that is released when they are cut and cooked. The mucilaginous quality is an essential component of some dishes. Okra are added to curries, stews, soups and gravies, but only in the last few minutes, unless the mucilaginous texture is an important part of the dish. Young fruits are high in vitamin C, carotene, calcium, magnesium, potassium and phosphate. Young shoots and leaves, flower buds and flowers are also eaten, usually steamed.

ERITREAN RECIPE FROM AESHA
Arabic Okra Casserole

1 teaspoon whole aniseed
1 teaspoon whole cloves
½ teaspoon whole white peppercorns
½ teaspoon whole black peppercorns
1 tablespoon oil
2 onions, chopped
½ tablespoon ground cumin
3 tomatoes, chopped and blended
½ cup water
500 g lamb, diced
1 teaspoon salt
300 g okra, topped and tailed
3–4 large cloves garlic, crushed

Crush the aniseed, cloves and black and white peppercorns using a mortar and pestle.

Add oil to a large pot and gently fry onions for 2 minutes. Add cumin and the crushed spices and continue to fry until onions are translucent. Add blended tomatoes and water to the onions and spices. Bring to the boil. Add lamb and salt. Simmer, covered, for ½ hour. Add okra and garlic and continue to simmer, covered, for 1½ hours until tender. Serve with rice or *injera* (see page 15). **Serves 4.**

Onions and shallots
Allium spp.

The main onions grown in the gardens are spring onions (A. *cepa*), Japanese bunching onions (A. *fistulosum*) and shallots (A. *cepa* Aggregatum Group). A few gardeners grow the common bulb onion. Spring and bunching onions are grown for their leaves and stems whereas shallots are grown for their bulbs as well. Japanese bunching onions are perennials that grow in large clumps with no obvious bulbs. Shallots grow from a single bulb that will divide into up to 20 segments as the shallots grow. Each segment produces tubular green leaves up to 40 cm in height. Shallots used in Asia usually have a purple or reddish skin and are often smaller than those seen in Europe.

Red shallots

Grow

Bunching and spring onions and small red shallots can be grown all over Australia from very cold mountainous regions to the sub-tropics. They do best in well-drained sandy loams with added compost and well-rotted manure. They need full sun, will tolerate fairly dry conditions and don't like to be waterlogged. Bulb onions grow best in the southern states. Grow new onion plants from seed that is best sown in seed trays and later transplanted, although they will grow from seed sown directly into the garden. Bunching onions can also be propagated by dividing existing clumps. Shallots are usually grown by planting individual bulbs, any time from autumn to early spring, with half the bulb protruding from the soil. Space them about 40 cm apart in rows the same distance apart. Harvest shallot bulbs in summer, while bunching and spring onions can be harvested all year round.

Garden talk

Both the leaves and stems of bunching onions are eaten. They have a mild, sweet, onion flavour early in the season but the flavour strengthens as the plant reaches maturity. Stems and leaves are commonly used in stir-fries and soups. Tju Ing chops spring onions and smells them to clear a blocked nose. Zeyneb chops them to add to salads and says that onions are an important ingredient of dolma (see page 143). Fatima also adds them to salads while Edite uses them in stir-fries. Both the bulbs and leaves of shallots are eaten. Bulbs are added to stir-fries and salads and the Vietnamese deep fry them until crisp and then use them as a garnish. Mai, Chue and Mor chop the bulbs and leaves of shallots, mix them with coriander leaves and add them to stir-fries.

GREEK RECIPE FROM DINA

TOURLOU (VEGETABLE DISH)

1 tablespoon olive oil
2 onions, chopped
2 sweet long tapered yellow-green capsicums, diced
220g fresh green beans, topped and tailed
1 green capsicum, diced
1 medium eggplant, diced
1 x 400g tin diced tomatoes
½ teaspoon salt
freshly ground black pepper
¼ cup water
2 tablespoons parsley, chopped

In a saucepan, put the olive oil and the onions and gently fry until soft. Add the yellow-green capsicums and the fresh beans and fry for a few more minutes. Add the green capsicum and continue to fry gently. Then add the eggplant and fry two minutes more. Now add the tinned tomatoes and bring to the boil, stirring occasionally. Season with salt and pepper and add the water and parsley. Bring to the boil again, then lower heat and simmer, uncovered, for 25–30 minutes. **Serves 2–4.**

ETHIOPIAN RECIPE FROM BASRA

LAMB CASSEROLE

1 tablespoon oil
500 g onions, sliced
500 g tomatoes, quartered
1 tablespoon chilli, finely chopped or ground with a mortar and pestle
2 teaspoons cumin powder
½ clove garlic, finely chopped or ground with a mortar and pestle
1 teaspoon salt
500 g lamb, cubed
5 potatoes, peeled and sliced

In a large pot, add oil and onions and gently fry until softened. Add tomatoes, chilli, cumin, garlic and salt, and continue to fry for a few minutes. Add the lamb, stir, and simmer, covered, until meat is tender. Add the sliced potatoes into the sauce and continue to simmer, covered, until potatoes are cooked but not mushy. Serve with rice. **Serves 4.**

Orach

Atriplex hortensis

Orach, also known as mountain spinach, is a hardy annual that grows tall and erect to over 1 m. The foliage is green, white or red, the red being the most popular in Australia. The green, white or red flowers and seeds grow in drooping spikes from the top of the plant.

Grow

Grow orach from seed sown in spring or summer into most soils, but the better the soil the more succulent the leaves. Plants self-sow readily. Orach likes full sun and reasonable water during dry periods but is really a pretty tough plant that survives most conditions.

Garden talk

The leaves are cooked and eaten in the same way as spinach, or young leaves and shoots can be eaten raw in salads and sandwiches. Georgia grows the red and green forms and boils the leaves of the green form like spinach but adds the red one to salad. She says she also uses the seeds for mustard.

Orach

Oregano

Origanum spp.

Oregano is a creeping perennial. The first leaves, which form a mat, are reddish, oval and slightly hairy; the later leaves are the same but green. Branched flowering stalks grow to 60 cm and are topped by pink or white flowers. There are numerous cultivars with varying flower and leaf colours.

Grow

Grow oregano from seed sown in spring or by taking cuttings or dividing clumps in spring or autumn. It likes full sun and will grow in most soils as long as they are very well drained.

Oregano

Garden talk

The strongly aromatic leaves are used to flavour meat dishes, sauces and stuffing. Julia dries oregano leaves for later use and Dina says, 'I use it a lot on roasts, lamb and chicken as well as with barbecued chops and I put oregano into the salad, salad is no good without oregano.' Alonzo adds oregano to vegetable chutneys made with cauliflower, carrots and vinegar. Leaves are strongly antiseptic so tea is made from the leaves to alleviate the symptoms of a cold and ease indigestion.

GREEK RECIPE FROM DINA

Greek Salad

1 cos lettuce, leaves torn
3 large tomatoes, cut into wedges
½ cucumber (telegraph), sliced
200g kalamata black olives, pitted
Greek fetta cheese, cubed
1 red onion, thinly sliced

Dressing
100 mL olive oil
100 mL white wine vinegar
1 teaspoon salt
1 tablespoon fresh oregano, finely chopped

Place all salad ingredients in a large bowl. Mix all dressing ingredients in a screw-top jar and shake well. Pour dressing over the salad and toss well. **Serves 4.**

Parsley

Petroselinum sativum

Parsley is a biennial that grows as a rosette of deeply divided dark green leaves to about 30 cm. Small yellow-green flowers grow in flower heads and these are followed by small, ribbed seeds. Italian or plain-leaf parsley is taller and has a stronger flavour.

Grow

Grow parsley from seed sown in spring or autumn. Seeds can take three to six weeks before they begin to grow. Plants prefer a humus-rich moist soil and a semi-shaded position. Cut back flower heads early in the second year to encourage more leaf growth, but later allow it to go to seed as it will self-sow prolifically.

Garden talk

Parsley is rich in vitamins, especially A and C, and contains several minerals including boron and fluorine which help keep bones strong. Fresh leaves are added to salads, sandwiches, soups, stews and stir-fries. Fiona uses a lot of parsley in her cooking, especially in

Curly parsley and Italian parsley

gremolata and tabouli. Vilma says that parsley should not be planted near mint, while Georgia explains that, 'You can make pesto from just parsley if you don't have the basil, because the parsley is there all year.' Medicinally, parsley helps to sweeten the breath; a tea made from the leaves aids digestion and eases gout and arthritis. Adelina drinks parsley tea to cleanse the bladder. 'I put a bunch in a half litre enamel pot, pour some really boiling water over it, cover it with a saucer and let it stand until it is just lukewarm.'

AUSTRALIAN RECIPE FROM FIONA
Gremolata

2 cups parsley, finely chopped
grated zest of 2 lemons
6 cloves garlic, crushed

Mix together all ingredients. Serve sprinkled over Osso Buco or other meat casseroles just before serving.

GREEK RECIPE FROM DINA
Keftepes

1 kg minced beef
2 cloves garlic, finely chopped
½ cup parsley, finely chopped
1 tablespoon mint, finely chopped
2 onions, finely chopped
1½ teaspoons salt
freshly ground black pepper to taste
4–5 slices stale bread, crusts removed and crumbled
2 eggs, lightly beaten
zest of 2 lemons
½ cup plain flour
olive oil for shallow frying

Combine all ingredients (except plain flour and olive oil) in a large bowl, and mix thoroughly. Using a heaped tablespoon of mixture, shape into a ball and roll in plain flour. Repeat until all the mixture is used. Flatten each meatball slightly.

In a large frying pan, heat 1–2 tablespoons olive oil and gently fry meatballs, turning once, until browned on both sides and cooked through. Remove and drain on paper towels. Serve hot or cold with salad. **Serves 6.**

Peas
Pisum sativum

Peas growing up an improvised trellis

The peas most commonly grown in the gardens are sugar snap peas and snow peas. These can be dwarf or climbing and produce peas with edible pods. Snow peas are best eaten when the peas are still very small while whole snap peas are still palatable when the peas are well developed.

Grow
Peas do best in an open, sunny position with a well-drained, fertile, deeply dug soil. Add manure and compost a few

SUDANESE RECIPE FROM RAWDA

Lamb and Vegetable Casserole

60 mL oil
2 onions, finely chopped
1 kg lamb, diced and soaked in salty water
2 x 400 g cans diced tomatoes
200 g sugar snap peas, topped and tailed
200 g fresh green beans, topped and tailed and chopped
into thirds
1 large carrot, sliced
2 potatoes, diced
2 cloves garlic, crushed

½ large eggplant, diced
½ cup red lentils
200 g fresh (or frozen) okra
4 teaspoons salt
2 teaspoons freshly ground black pepper
3 teaspoons cinnamon
2 tablespoons parsley, finely chopped
4 teaspoons whole fennel seed
4 teaspoons ground coriander seed
2 tablespoons mint, chopped

Pour oil into a large pot. Add onions and brown, stirring. Add drained lamb and brown. Add diced tomatoes and stir. Lower heat and cover with a lid. Cook for a few minutes. Add all other ingredients and simmer gently, covered, until cooked (approximately 1½ hours). Check seasonings and serve. **Serves 4–6.**

weeks before planting. Plant peas directly into the soil where they are to grow from January to October, 10 cm apart in rows 50 cm apart.

Garden talk
Peas are grown in many of the gardens, using vertical spaces like fences, tripods and trellises to increase the garden area. They are eaten on their own or added to salads, soups, stews and stir-fries. Young leaves, shoots and flowers are all eaten and the seeds are sprouted and the sprouts eaten in salads and stir-fries.

Pepino

Solanum muricatum

These South American perennials grow as small bushes to 1 m with glossy, oval to lance-shaped leaves and purple or white and purple flowers. The flowers are followed by white or pale green ovoid fruit with purple markings. The fruit has yellow flesh that tastes like melon.

Grow
Pepinos do well in a humus-rich soil in full sun with plenty of water. They will not tolerate frosts. Add some well-rotted manure in spring. Harvest fruit in autumn but only when the fruit is fully mature, has developed a fragrance and has just started to soften and turn yellow. Fruit harvested too early has

Pepino

an unpleasant after-taste. Bushes only last a few years, so take cuttings in spring to grow new plants to replace old ones.

Garden talk

This plant is a native of South America and is commonly seen in gardens of people from that region. The small melon is eaten fresh, just peeled and cut into slices. The flavour is sweet and aromatic. It is also added to fruit salads and goes particularly well with citrus. Fruit are made into jams, jellies, preserves and sauces. Pepinos are also added to savoury dishes like soup and salsa.

Perilla

Perilla frutescens

Perilla is a fast-growing annual that reaches about 80 cm. It forms a compact shrub with large, oval leaves with serrated edges, and spikes of small white or mauve flowers. There is a variety with green leaves, and another, more widely available, with crinkled red-magenta leaves.

Grow

Grow perilla from seed sown in spring or autumn, where it is to grow. Thin to about 25 cm between plants. Perilla grows best in a sunny position with well-drained soil to which compost and well-rotted manure has been added. In regions with very hot, dry summers, grow where it is protected from the hot afternoon sun.

Garden talk

Leaves have a flavour reminiscent of lemon, mint, cloves and basil. Leaves are added to salads and soups, eaten fresh in spring rolls and used to wrap grilled meats. Shu Xian serves steamed crab or fish on a bed of perilla leaves and says that it removes the strong 'bad' taste. So and Ruyet say that perilla can only be eaten raw, not cooked and Thiep mixes perilla with mint and lettuce and says it is good for back pain. Medicinally, a strong infusion of the leaves is used to reduce a temperature. Tai adds it to soup that he says is good for colds and flu.

Perilla

North Melbourne Community Garden

Plantain
Plantago major

Large or common plantain is naturalised through most of the world. This perennial grows in a clump as a low rosette of long oval leaves. Each leaf blade has five to nine conspicuous longitudinal veins. The flowers are tiny and yellow-green.

Grow
In Australia plantains are found growing wild in gardens and public spaces. They prefer sandy or loamy, moist, nutrient-rich soil and are grown easily from seed.

Garden talk
Julia knows this herb as *llantén* and says it is good for diabetes and to put on a bruise. 'Just break it up in pieces like that and put it on top. You can put it in salad too.' Medicinally, plantain kills a wide range of micro-organisms and stimulates healing. Rub a leaf onto a bite or sting to reduce swelling and pain.

Plantain

Potato
Solanum tuberosum

This short-lived perennial has hundreds of cultivars with different coloured skins and flesh. Mauve pink flowers are followed by green berries that turn purple and are poisonous.

Grow
New potato plants are grown from the tubers of old plants. Any potatoes left in the ground will re-shoot the following year. Potatoes do best in a very humus-rich, deeply dug soil with well-rotted manure dug in several weeks before planting. They like full sun. Plant tubers from September to January about 30 cm apart. Harvest between four and five months later.

Potato

Garden talk

Potatoes can be fried, boiled, mashed, roasted, baked and eaten hot or cold. Different cultivars are better for different forms of cooking. Sophie likes to serve potatoes with lemon and oregano. She has tried growing two different varieties and says the Desirée potatoes were beautiful. 'They tasted like they've got sugar in them.' Adelina says, 'I love it when my potatoes are in blossom and they have beautiful lilac and pink flowers. It is gorgeous.'

AUSTRALIAN RECIPE FROM COREY
POTATO WITH CHEESY TOPPING

6 potatoes
1 onion, finely sliced
½ capsicum, finely chopped
1 cup milk (or cream)
½ cup fresh parsley, finely chopped
1 chilli, seeded and finely chopped
½ cup spinach, finely chopped
1 cup tasty cheese, grated

Pre-heat oven to 350°F (180°C). Parboil potatoes, then slice. Mix all ingredients together (except cheese) and place in a baking dish. Sprinkle grated cheese on top.

Bake in oven for 15–20 minutes until cheese is melted and golden brown. **Serves 4–6** as an accompaniment.

AUSTRALIAN RECIPE FROM ASSI
SHEPHERD'S PIE

1 tablespoon olive oil
1 onion, chopped
3 carrots, thickly sliced
½ large head broccoli, cut into florets
450 g broad beans
1 clove garlic, crushed
2 teaspoons salt
½ teaspoon freshly ground black pepper
2 teaspoons dried basil
2 bay leaves
4 tablespoons tomato paste
2 cups water
6 medium potatoes, peeled
1 teaspoon butter
200 mL milk
2–3 tomatoes, sliced
tasty cheese, sliced

Preheat oven 350°F (180°C). Put the olive oil in a large saucepan and gently fry the onion until soft and translucent. Add carrots, broccoli, broad beans and garlic and cook for a further 5 minutes. Add 1 teaspoon salt, pepper, basil, bay leaves, tomato paste and water, stir through, then cover and simmer for 30 minutes, stirring occasionally.

In a separate saucepan, place potatoes and cover with hot water. Add 1 teaspoon salt, and simmer, covered, until cooked. Drain and mash, add butter, and slowly stir in the milk until smooth and creamy.

Spoon vegetable mixture into a non-metal baking dish, not including excess liquid. Evenly spread mashed potato over the mix and top with sliced tomatoes, then sliced tasty cheese. Bake in the oven until bubbling and cheese has melted and browned. **Serves 2.**

Purple rice plant
Peristrophe speciosa

Purple rice plant

This tropical perennial plant grows as a small shrub to about 1 m. It has glossy, dark green oval leaves and violet to magenta flowers in summer.

Grow

Purple rice plant will grow in any reasonable, humus-rich soil with good drainage. It is a tropical plant, so needs plenty of water and lots of warmth but also protection from the very hot sun in the middle of summer. In cooler regions, move inside or into a warm, sheltered position in winter. Grow from seed sown in spring or by taking tip cuttings in late spring.

Garden talk

Purple rice plant gets its name from its use in colouring foods. The leaves are boiled in water to give a purple liquid. This liquid is then used to cook rice, which turns purple, or to colour cooked eggs, biscuits and rice desserts. Thai uses purple rice plant, which she calls *la cam*. 'When you cook it with the sticky rice the colour comes out beautifully, the rice is purple.' Thiep says that the leaf looks green but when you cook it the colour changes to purple. 'In winter we have to cover them or dig them up and put into pots and take them to the flat to keep them alive. When the winter is over, we bring them back here.'

Purslane
Portulaca oleracea

Purslane

Purslane is a succulent, sprawling annual that is a weed in high rainfall areas. It has smooth reddish stems and clusters of small succulent leaves, which are dark green with a red line around the edge. Flowers are yellow.

Grow

Grow from seed sown in spring into any reasonable soil. Plants can become weedy and will self-sow readily. Grow in full sun or semi-shade.

Garden talk

The succulent leaves and young shoots of purslane are added to salads, soups and sandwiches. It has been used medicinally to prevent scurvy. Ibrahim says that purslane, which he calls *regla*, is a very useful plant. He usually cooks it, especially in a salsa made with meat and tomato. Aesha chops it with the stem and cooks it very slowly with onion, oil, tomato, meat and hot pepper. Sitina uses purslane in salad but also cooks it. Fiona says, 'I had a big patch of purslane and it is a really delicious vegetable. Wash it very carefully and then braise it with a little oil and garlic for about 10 minutes and that gives a really nice gluey, chewy, sort of vegetable that I like. You can also eat it raw in a salad.' Rawda calls this plant *baqla* and likes to cook it with lentils.

Radish

Raphanus sativus

Black radish

This annual vegetable grows as a clump of narrow, dark green leaves with a long, cylindrical, oblong or spherical root. Radishes fall into three main groups, all of which are grown in the gardens. European radish roots can be pink, red, purple, white, yellow and black skinned. They vary in shape from small round balls to long and tapering. Japanese radish roots (*daikon*) are all white (some with a tinge of green) and mostly long and tapering. Their leaves are generally inedible. Chinese radish roots (*lo bok*) have green, red and white skins and vary from round to long and tapering. The flesh is often sweet and the leaves are usually edible.

Grow

Radishes are grown from seed that can be planted at any time of the year. Sow seed direct into shallow drills 2 cm deep. They prefer a deep, rich, light, well-drained and well-cultivated soil, especially if the long tapering varieties are grown. Add manure and compost a few weeks before planting. Regular water is important because roots must grow rapidly if they are to be mild and tender.

Garden talk

The use varies with the type. Many radishes are eaten raw in salads or just on their own like an apple. Some, like Japanese radishes, are usually cooked while Chinese radishes are both cooked and eaten raw. The leaves are eaten as a vegetable, steamed or stir-fried, and young flower heads are treated in the same way. The whole plant is rich in carotene and calcium. Kapitolina grows black radishes and says that they are good for colds. Lioudmila agrees that they are very healthy. She combines them with honey and onions, 'If you have bronchitis, it is very, very strong. It just clears the phlegm.'

ETHIOPIAN RECIPE FROM TAWFIK

Fresh Salad

2 radishes, finely sliced
½ lettuce, torn
½ bunch coriander, chopped
1 fresh red chilli, finely chopped and seeded

Dressing
1 tablespoon olive oil
1 tablespoon lemon juice

Place all the salad ingredients in a large bowl. Place the dressing ingredients in a screw-top jar and shake well. Add dressing to the salad and toss well. **Serves 2.**

RUSSIAN RECIPE FROM LIOUDMILA

Health Improving Radish Remedy

1 black radish
2 tablespoons honey
juice of 1 lemon

Peel the radish and then grate into a bowl using a coarse grater. Mix the honey in with the radish and leave to stand for at least three hours. Strain the liquid through a piece of gauze into a jar, squeezing to extract as much liquid as possible. Add the lemon juice. Seal the jar and store in the refrigerator. Take one tablespoon after meals to help keep you healthy, and whenever needed for coughs and bronchitis.

Rocket

Eruca sativa

Rocket is an annual that grows from 30–70 cm high depending on soil and climate. It has dark green, indented leaves and purplish stems. The flowers are cream or white with purplish veins.

Grow

Propagate rocket from seed sown in spring and summer. It self-sows readily. Rocket does best in a humus-rich, well-drained soil in full sun or semi-shade, but is really a tough, trouble free plant that will grow in most conditions. Start harvesting leaves as soon as plants are big enough.

Garden talk

The leaves have a strong pungent flavour that becomes more bitter when the plant flowers. It is widely

Rocket

grown in the gardens of people from the Mediterranean and African regions. Basra uses rocket in salads; she just washes it first. Aesha and Fatima call this plant *jiir jiir* and both add it to salad too. Leaves are also eaten in sandwiches and dips.

Rue

Ruta graveolens

Rue is an attractive perennial herb that grows as a bush to 1 m with deeply divided, blue-green leaves and yellow flowers.

Grow

Grow from seed sown in spring or cuttings taken in spring or summer. Rue seems to do best in poor dry soil but generally tolerates most soils and does well in full sun and semi-shade.

Garden talk

Rue is used medicinally, as a spice in cooking and to repel pests. It is a strong herb so should always be used with care. Some people are allergic to it so always wear gloves when handling. Vilma says that rue is good for lots of things. 'It is a great medicine. As a drink it is good for flatulence and hiccups and if you have a stomach-ache. It is even used to frighten bad spirits off.' Alonzo calls this plant *rudz* and rubs the leaves on the body to reduce pain. Fatima says they make a tea from the leaves of rue, which she calls *talatam*, for stomach-ache and headache, and they rub the chopped and crushed leaves on the body to bring the temperature down. They also use rue in cooking. 'We dry the seeds and put with ginger, chilli and garlic and make a paste. It is very strong and smells nice. We put it into meat or chicken casseroles.' Fiona also grows rue. 'I use it with coffee, that is a trick an Ethiopian friend taught me, its an acquired taste, but when you get used to it, it really tastes terrific.'

Rue

Sage

Sage

Salvia officinalis

Common sage grows to about 50 cm and has woody stems, oblong grey-green leaves that are soft and hairy, and blue-purple flowers that grow in spikes. It is a short-lived perennial.

Grow

Grow sage from seed sown in spring, by taking cuttings in late spring, or by layering older bushes in winter. Sage will grow in most soils as long as they are well drained and plants get full sun.

Garden talk

Sage is used medicinally and in cooking, particularly in stuffings, with cheese, and as part of a *bouquet garni* in stews, soups and casseroles. Sage is strongly antiseptic and recent research suggests that sage is also anti-oxidant and may even slow ageing and improve memory. Georgia makes sage tea by boiling leaves in water. She adds honey and says that it is very healthy. 'It is good for everything. For cancer, for laryngitis to make a gargle, especially for colds, for many, many things.'

Silver beet

Beta vulgaris Cicla Group

A mass of young silver beet seedlings

Silver beet, also known as Swiss chard, is a biennial or perennial that grows as a dense clump of succulent stems that can be white, red, yellow, orange or purple, with wavy glossy green leaves.

Grow

Silver beet will grow in most soils and most positions but prefers full sun to semi-shade and a compost-enriched, well-drained soil with adequate water during dry periods. Top dress with manures to encourage leafy growth. Grow new plants from seed sown July to March.

TURKISH RECIPE FROM ZEYNEB

Stuffed Silver Beet Dolmas

1 large bunch silver beet, stalks and central vein removed so that leaves are cut in half
500 g minced beef or lamb
2 cups uncooked rice
1 onion
2 tablespoons tomato paste
1 tablespoon margarine
1 tomato, finely diced
1 chilli, finely chopped
1 teaspoon salt
1 teaspoon freshly ground black pepper
1 tablespoon chicken stock powder
½ bunch parsley, finely chopped
½ bunch mint, finely chopped
chicken stock to cover

Wash and pat dry the silver beet leaves. In a large bowl, mix together all other ingredients except the chicken stock. Put a small amount of this stuffing in each leaf and carefully roll up, tucking ends in as you roll. Place rolls in a large pot, cover with chicken stock, and simmer gently, covered, until meat is cooked and leaves are soft (approximately 20 minutes). **Serves 4.**

SUDANESE RECIPE FROM RAWDA

SILVER BEET WITH TOMATO AND ONION

1 tablespoon oil
1 onion, finely chopped
2 tomatoes, diced
1 clove garlic, crushed
½ teaspoon salt
½ teaspoon freshly ground black pepper
¼ teaspoon ground cinnamon
½ teaspoon whole fennel seeds
½ teaspoon ground coriander seeds
4 cups silver beet leaves, finely shredded

Add oil into a medium sized saucepan. Gently fry onion until soft. Add the rest of the ingredients, except the silver beet. Continue to cook gently, uncovered, for a further 5 minutes, stirring occasionally, until well softened. Add silver beet on top of the mixture, cover with a lid, and lower heat. Allow to cook until silver beet is wilted. Stir well so the silver beet is mixed through, and serve. **Serves 2.**

Garden talk

Silver beet is such an easy to grow, prolific plant that it is seen right through the gardens. Julia uses it to make tortilla and says it is all vitamins, pure vitamins. Vilma and Thiep both add it to soup while Zeyneb uses it to make dolmas. Sometimes Fatima will just steam silver beet but she also likes to combine it with zucchini, onion and garlic and cook it with lasagne. Kerama says that silver beet is good for the stomach. 'If there is a tummy ache boil it, drain the water and add a little oil and lemon juice and salt and eat it and it will fix up your stomach.' Rawda cooks it with tomato and onion and Georgia uses it in all sorts of dishes, especially spanakopita (see page 106). 'I love silver beet because the silver beet really, really helps me. You cut the leaves and it comes again, cut and comes again.'

Sorrel

Sorrel

Rumex acetosa

Garden sorrel has oval matt-green leaves that are twice as long as they are wide. It grows as a clump to about 70 cm and the flowers are reddish-green.

Grow

Sorrel is grown by dividing clumps in spring or autumn, or sowing seed in spring. It grows best in compost-enriched soil in full sun with adequate water. Remove flowering stems to encourage leaf growth.

Garden talk

The leaves have a sour lemony taste. Kapitolina says that sorrel is not as famous here as it is in Russia, but that it makes a beautiful soup. She adds that sorrel is at its best in spring. Fiona likes sorrel for its acidic taste and adds it to salads as well as putting a sprig in a cup and pouring her cup of coffee over it. 'It really enhances the taste. Not every time but for a special treat or when my friends come to visit.'

Strawberry

Fragaria spp.

Ida's strawberries with little supports made by Mendel

The commonly cultivated garden strawberry (*F.* × *ananassa*) has a spreading habit, oval leaflets, white flowers and typical red fruit. Wild strawberry (*F. vesca*) has a more vigorous spreading habit, with smaller fruit while the alpine strawberry (*F. vesca* 'Semperflorens') is a runnerless cultivar which grows in a compact clump with small tear-shaped fruit, usually red, although they can be yellow or white. Their flavour is true strawberry with undertones of blackberry.

Grow

Grow strawberries from seed sown in spring or summer; some forms will self-sow readily. Alternatively grow new plants by detaching rooted pieces or by dividing clumps. Strawberries like a humus-rich soil with full sun and plenty of water when the fruit are setting. They grow well in pots.

Garden talk

Many of the gardeners grow strawberries, often in pots next to their garden beds, but Ida is the most passionate. She really loves her bush strawberries (they are probably a form of alpine strawberry). 'I was eating these strawberries all summer through. They are very, very important and it is very difficult to preserve them. People from Russia and the Ukraine they know about the qualities of these berries but other people do not know. There is one more secret I would like to share with you. The strawberries, when they are in blossom, you put a little bit around of the leaves from the Christmas tree. Not a lot.' Ida adds that she wants to plant garlic, but that strawberries don't like garlic, so she is not sure if she will.

Sweet potato

Ipomoea batatas

Sweet potato is a perennial plant that is usually grown as an annual. It grows from underground tuberous roots with trailing, twisting stems that can be 6 m long. Leaves are generally heart-shaped. Roots grow from stem nodes as they touch the ground, and most of these grow into more tubers. Up to eight tubers can be produced on each plant. The flesh of the tubers can be white, yellow, purple, red, orange and brown. White-fleshed varieties tend to be less sweet than the others.

Grow

Sweet potatoes are grown from seeds, cuttings or by planting tubers. They do best in full sun in a fertile, open, sandy soil with some added manure and compost. Plant each tuber about 1 m from the next. Sweet potatoes usually need four to five frost-free months in order to produce tubers of a reasonable size, although there are some cultivars that will produce tubers in as little as three months. Sweet potatoes are regarded as a tropical crop, but they can be grown in the summer in temperate regions although most will not usually produce useful tubers.

Garden talk

Sweet potatoes are mainly grown for their leaves in the gardens, although some gardeners do manage to grow tubers too. Tubers are boiled, baked and fried. Young leaves and the tips of the vines are also boiled and eaten; they are high in protein and vitamin C. Mrs Poon says that she eats the leaves by frying them. 'If you want to grow them pick one up and just stick it into the soil and it will take root.' Niu Jia maintains that in China the leaves are pig fodder only. 'I am growing it just for fun. I don't know if I will eat the leaves. The other gardeners have said if you fry it (the leaves) it is very delicious so I have just grown a little bit to try.' Edite explains how to prepare the leaves. 'We peel the skin from the stem, and then you wash it and cook it in the stir-fry with the leaves as well.' Tju Ing remembers that when she lived in East Timor they would preserve the leaves by partly drying them in the sun, then mixing them with salt, putting them in a jar and adding water. 'I would keep it for maybe a week. When it turns yellow it is ready to use. I don't preserve them any more. Sometimes I make a little bit just for our own use.' She also adds sweet potato leaves to ginger, garlic, meat and soy sauce all mixed together and fried

Sweet potato leaves

Taro

Colocasia esculenta

A perennial plant, taro grows from tuberous roots with erect purple or green stems that can be over a metre high. The purple or green oval leaves can be very large, resembling elephant ears. Flowers are green and yellow and followed by green berries.

Grow

Taro does well in most soils as long as they are nutrient-rich and acid to neutral. It is a heavy feeder so add manure before planting. Grow new plants by planting tubers so they are covered by about 6 cm of soil about 35 cm apart. Water liberally and add more manure when plants are about 60 cm high. Taro is a tropical or sub-tropical plant that must have a long hot summer to develop large tubers. It does not tolerate heavy frosts. It is not usually possible to grow plump, edible taro tubers in cool climates because it is not hot enough for long enough. Taro is an attractive plant in its own right and by choosing the right cultivars can be grown simply for its stems and leaves. These are harvested at any time, but are at their best in spring and summer.

Garden talk

Never eat taro raw, as all parts contain calcium oxalate, which is made up of sharp crystals that cause intense irritation to the inside of the mouth and tongue. This dissipates with cooking. Modern cultivars have very low calcium oxalate content, and most of this is found in the skin, so always peel tubers and stems before cooking. Some cultivars of taro are grown specifically for their stems rather than the tubers. Eat only young leaves and always boil leaves and stems before eating. In warmer climates taro is mostly grown for its

Taro

tubers; these can be roasted, fried, baked, braised, mashed, or boiled. Thiep skins taro stems and then cooks them in sour fish soup (see page 108). Ana uses the root, stems and leaves but says that you sometimes have to leave the plants for two years to get a good-sized root. 'Don't take the leaves, leave the root to grow. When I harvest the root I use the leaves, the stem everything. We cook the leaves and stem with tamarind, corn – anything you want.' She goes on to explain that when they were farming and someone cut themselves they would treat it with taro. 'Peel the stem and use the peel as a bandaid. It has healing qualities and helps to keep the flies away.' Pherina grows large quantities of taro, but only for the leaves because it doesn't grow proper roots here. 'Peta (the garden worker) said to get straw and put it all around so it won't be so dry underneath, because taro can't be dry.' When they harvested the leaves and divided the roots to replant, some of the neighbouring gardeners asked for the bits of roots they didn't want. 'We throw that part away because to us it is no good; they come the other day and took it all, they said we eat it, we make chips out of it.' Pherina explains how to cook the leaves. 'We boil the leaves but you've got to change the water maybe 2 or 3 times because if you don't cook it right it gets really itchy. But if you bake it you don't need to change any water, so that is different. Just roll the meat in the leaves, put coconut cream on it so it doesn't get too dry and put it in the oven and cover in foil. It's beautiful. I never used to like it but now I love it.'

Tomato

Lycopersicon esculentum

Tomato

Tomatoes are probably the most widely grown vegetable in Australia. There are hundreds of varieties varying in plant and fruit size, colour and flavour.

Grow

Tomatoes are annuals that grow in most soils as long as they are well drained. They like full sun and need to be protected against late frosts. Enrich the soil with manure a few weeks before planting and water with a complete fertiliser soon after planting, and again when flowers first appear. Don't use fertilisers high in nitrogen as this will encourage leaf growth at the expense of flowers and fruit. Grow from seed sown in early spring, under glass in temperate regions, or from seedlings planted out after the last chance of frost is over. Tall varieties need to be staked, smaller varieties do well in large pots.

Garden talk

Tomatoes are used in salads and sauces, as well as sandwiches, dips, stir-fries, stews and soups. Ida loves to grow Black Russian tomatoes, some yellow German ones and others with stripes. Rawda grows a couple of different varieties, including Roma, and found that some of her last year's crop self-seeded and grew again this year. Ana likes to grow big tomatoes and tries to save her own seed from year to year. 'In Timor the tomatoes just grow wild, the cherry tomatoes and the big tomatoes just grow all over the place.' Dina had trouble with the sparrows attacking her tomatoes so she collected all her plastic bags and tied one around each tomato. Georgia grows ox heart tomatoes and says the largest one she has picked was 600 grams. When she cooks her tomatoes she adds a lot of basil and a little bit of salt and says that this time she put garlic too, but not too much. Sophie loves the fresh tomatoes. 'The tomatoes from the supermarket are tasteless. No taste, nothing. They are best from the garden.' Oscar experimented with growing new tomatoes from cuttings of the old plant and found that they grew well.

GREEK RECIPE FROM SOPHIE
STUFFED TOMATOES AND CAPSICUMS

6 large tomatoes
6 large green capsicums
2 tablespoons tomato paste
½ teaspoon sugar
1 cup olive oil
750 g minced beef or lamb
1 large eggplant, peeled and diced
1 cup onions, finely chopped
2 teaspoons salt
2 teaspoons freshly ground black pepper
½ cup uncooked medium grain rice
½ cup parsley, finely chopped
1 tablespoon mint, finely chopped
1 tablespoon dried oregano
2 large potatoes
1 tablespoon butter or margarine
juice of 2 lemons

Preheat the oven to 350°F (180°C). Wash the tomatoes and capsicums thoroughly. Cut the top off each tomato, horizontally, to form a lid and scoop the seeds out into a bowl. Insert a pinch of salt in each tomato and turn them upside down to drain. Follow the same procedure with the capsicums but discard the seeds. Blend the tomato seeds and tomato paste together and add the sugar.

In a large frying pan, pour ½ cup oil. Add the minced meat, eggplant and onion, and fry on high heat for 15 minutes. Add the tomato blend and salt and pepper and gently fry for a further 15 minutes. Take the pan off the heat and stir in the rice, parsley, mint and oregano. Stuff the capsicums and tomatoes with the mixture and place in a deep baking dish. Replace the lids on top of the tomatoes and capsicums.

Wash and cut the potatoes into large wedges (4 or 6 pieces depending on the size of the potatoes) and place them vertically between the tomatoes and the capsicums. Season with a little extra salt and pepper and dot with butter or margarine.

Pour the remaining olive oil on top of the tomatoes and capsicums. Squeeze the lemon juice over the potatoes. Bake (uncovered) in the oven for 1 ½ hours until the capsicums and tomatoes are well browned. **Serves 6** as a main meal.

GREEK RECIPE FROM MARIA
CHICKEN OR BEEF SCHNITZEL

Tomato Sauce
3 tomatoes, diced
1 onion, finely chopped
½ teaspoon salt
¼ teaspoon freshly ground black pepper

Schnitzels
2–3 eggs
1 tablespoon milk
¼ teaspoon fresh fine leafed basil, finely chopped
¼ teaspoon fresh oregano, finely chopped
1 tablespoon parsley, finely chopped
1 pinch freshly ground black pepper
¼ teaspoon salt
1 clove garlic, crushed
4 schnitzels (chicken or beef)
plain flour mixed with extra ¼ teaspoon salt and ⅛ teaspoon pepper, spread on a dinner plate
dried breadcrumbs, spread on a dinner plate
olive oil
mozzarella cheese

Preheat oven to 400°F (200°C).

Make the tomato sauce by combining the tomatoes, onion, salt and pepper in a small saucepan. Bring to the boil, stirring, then lower heat and simmer, covered, until soft and mushy. Remove lid and continue to simmer until most of the liquid has evaporated. Keep warm.

In a large bowl, whisk together the eggs, milk, basil, oregano, parsley, salt, pepper and garlic. Place the schnitzels in this mixture and marinate for 10 minutes to absorb the flavours. Remove schnitzels from mixture and coat well in flour. Next put schnitzels back into egg mixture, then coat well in breadcrumbs.

In a large non-stick frying pan, add 2 tablespoons oil and, over medium heat, fry the schnitzels until golden on both sides. Remove to a plate covered with absorbent paper until all the schnitzels are cooked. Place cooked schnitzels in an ovenproof dish and cover with a generous amount of tomato sauce. Sprinkle liberally with mozzarella cheese and heat in oven until cheese melts. Serve immediately. **Serves 4.**

Vietnamese balm
Elsholtzia ciliata

Vietnamese balm

Vietnamese balm is an annual that grows to about 1 m with bright green, pointed, serrated, oval leaves with a sharp lemon-mint fragrance and flavour. The stems are square with a deep red tinge. Flowers are pale purple.

Grow

Grow from seed or cuttings taken in spring. In warm climates the stems will root in water. Sow seed into trays and transplant to about 50 cm apart once seedlings are big enough to handle. Vietnamese balm likes most soils as long as they are well drained, and will grow in full sun or semi-shade. Top-dress with compost and manure, and water with liquid seaweed once a month or so during the growing season. Keep the flower heads cut back to encourage leaf growth.

Garden talk

Mien eats Vietnamese balm leaves on their own or mixes them with lettuce. She also puts them on top of beef soup or noodles. She says the leaves can be dried in the sun too, for later use. 'I put it into the pot, put the water in and then boil it. I drink it every day. It keeps me healthy. And we use it for a cough or anyone who has a headache, or high temperature or flu.' Ruyet also eats the leaves raw, either with other vegies or on their own, and agrees they are very good for your health. She grows new plants from seed or from cuttings and says that most will die in winter but if you cut them back and cover them then you may be able to keep some alive for next season.

Vietnamese mint
Persicaria odorata

Vietnamese mint

This sprawling plant grows in a clump with many-jointed stems to a height of 80 cm. The leaves are lance-shaped and bright green with reddish-brown markings. These markings often disappear in winter or when the plant is grown in a shady position. The small flowers are pink and the whole plant has a pungent scent and hot flavour.

Grow

Vietnamese mint is best grown from cuttings that will root in soil or water, or by detaching the outside stems that have sent out new roots where they have touched the soil. Space plants about 40 cm apart. It will not tolerate frosts, so in very cold regions grow as an annual or in a pot so that it can be moved inside in winter. It likes a fertile soil with plenty of water, and will grow well on the edge of a pond, doing best in shade or semi-shade.

Garden talk
The leaves of Vietnamese mint have a hot, peppery taste and the older the leaves, the hotter the flavour. It is an essential ingredient of many Vietnamese dishes, and is often sprinkled over fried chicken and chicken soups. Fiona uses Vietnamese mint when she is making laksa (spicy soup) and chicken curry. 'I probably use about ten leaves of Vietnamese mint in a laksa. Quite a lot because I love the taste. Then of course you can also use it for salads.' Mai, Chue and Mor use Vietnamese mint with fish. 'We chop it finely and mix with the fish and steam.'

Water celery
Oenanthe javanica

Water celery

Water celery grows from branching, erect, angled stems with oval, deeply divided leaves to about 40 cm. Flowers are tiny and white.

Grow
Water celery grows easily from seed or cuttings, with small pieces growing roots if left standing in a glass of water. It likes a good, composted soil enriched with manure and can be grown in any container that holds water. Cover the soil with about 10 cm of water and plant the water celery firmly into the soil and place in a sunny or semi-shaded position. Top up with fresh water at least once a week. This plant spreads rapidly, so thin out once a year if the pot becomes too crowded. It will easily colonise marshy areas, so make sure it doesn't escape into the wild.

Garden talk
Stems and leaves are eaten fresh in salads and added at the last minute to soups and stir-fries. They can also be steamed briefly and served as a vegetable with soy sauce. The whole plant has a strong celery flavour. Raw, finely chopped leaves are stirred into rice to give it a delicious celery flavour. Mien adds water celery when she stir-fries beef, putting it in just before taking the dish off the heat. 'Vietnamese use it for high blood pressure so just cook it and eat it and it brings the blood pressure down.' Ruyet eats water celery raw or fries it with beef, pork, chicken, prawns or calamari but not fish.

VIETNAMESE RECIPE FROM RUYET

STIR-FRIED BEEF WITH WATER CELERY ·

150 g fillet steak, thinly sliced
1 onion, finely chopped
2 teaspoons arrowroot powder
1½ tablespoons fish sauce
2 tablespoons vegetable oil
2 cloves garlic, crushed
1 bunch water celery, washed and cut into 5 cm pieces
1 teaspoon freshly ground black pepper
1 red chilli, seeded and finely chopped
1 tomato, sliced

In a bowl, mix together the steak, onion, arrowroot and ½ tablespoon fish sauce.

Heat oil in a large non-stick frying pan or wok. Add garlic and stir-fry briefly. Add steak mixture and stir-fry, over high heat, for 1 minute. Add water celery and stir-fry for 3 minutes. Add remaining fish sauce, pepper, chilli and tomato and stir-fry an extra 2 minutes. **Serves 4.**

VIETNAMESE RECIPE FROM RUYET

WATER CELERY SALAD WITH BEEF

Dressing
1½ tablespoons rice vinegar
4½ tablespoons water
1 tablespoon sugar
¼ teaspoon salt

200 g fillet steak, thinly sliced
1 tablespoon fish sauce
½ bunch water celery, trimmed of tough bottom stalks, rinsed well and torn into bite sized lengths
1 tomato, sliced
1 tablespoon vegetable oil
1 onion, thinly sliced
2 cloves garlic, thinly sliced
1 hot red chilli, seeded and finely chopped
1 teaspoon sugar
2 tablespoons water

Place all dressing ingredients in a screw-top jar and shake well. Set aside.

In a bowl, mix together the steak and fish sauce, and marinate for 30 minutes.

Divide water celery between 2 plates. Place slices of tomato on top of water celery. Sprinkle salad with a little dressing and set aside.

In a large wok, add oil. Gently stir-fry onion, garlic and chilli until softened. Add sugar, and stir well until slightly caramelised. Add steak, marinade and water and stir-fry until just coloured. Divide in two, place on top of salads and serve immediately. **Serves 2.**

Water chestnuts

Eleocharis dulcis

A water plant that grows naturally on the edges of swamps and waterways, water chestnuts are perennials with narrow, tubular, upright leaves. Insignificant flowers form at the tips of the stems. They grow from spreading rhizomes that sucker and produce new plants and corms during the growing season.

Grow

Grow water chestnuts in a pond or container that will hold water. An old bath is ideal. They like a reasonably rich soil with plenty of nutrients. Give any added manure a couple of weeks to rot before the corms are planted. The soil needs to be about 30 cm deep. Plant corms about 30 cm apart, 4 cm below the surface of the soil with the growth buds at the top. Water well, but do not flood. When plants are growing strongly increase the water level to 10–20 cm above the soil. Chestnut corms begin to swell as the days get shorter in autumn. At the same time the stems above water begin to brown off and die. Harvest corms from winter to early spring.

Garden talk

Water chestnuts are grown right through the gardens by Chinese and Vietnamese gardeners. They mostly grow them in a white foam box lined with black plastic. Water chestnuts are prepared by washing carefully, trimming the top and the bottom and then removing the skin. They are eaten raw or added to salads as well as savoury and sweet dishes, where they are valued for the sweet flavour and crisp, crunchy texture. They are an important ingredient of many chop suey dishes and are particularly good in vegetable stir-fries.

Water chestnuts and arrowhead growing in a polystyrene box

Dahlia's, chillies, fish plant and perilla grow side by side in one garden.

Watercress

Rorippa nasturtium-aquaticum

A much-branched, aquatic, perennial plant, watercress has a low, creeping growth habit, with heart-shaped, bright green leaflets and white flowers. Roots grow from nodes where they touch the ground.

Grow

Ideally watercress should be grown in running water, but it survives well in a pond with soil in the bottom that is topped up regularly with fresh water; or in a pot sitting in another container full of water that is also regularly topped up. Watercress likes a humus-rich, fertile soil and full sun. Grow it from seed sown in spring, or from rooted pieces. A piece of watercress left standing in a glass of water will grow roots in a couple of weeks. Once plants are established remove any flower heads to promote leaf growth and prolong harvest.

Garden talk

Young shoots and leaves are eaten in salads and used as a garnish. The Vietnamese call this plant *xa lach xoong*, which means little lettuce, and they eat it fresh with other salad greens, and add it to soups just before serving. The Chinese people fry watercress with fish or pork. Watercress is high in vitamins A, B1, B2, C and E as well as calcium, copper, iron and magnesium. Thiep uses watercress to make soup and serves it with fried beef salad.

Watercress

VIETNAMESE RECIPE FROM TRI

Beef and Watercress Salad

Dressing
¼ teaspoon salt
1 tablespoon sugar
1½ tablespoons rice vinegar
4½ tablespoons water

3 cloves garlic, finely sliced
1 tablespoon fish sauce
1½ teaspoons sugar
3 tablespoons vegetable oil
250 g fillet steak, thinly sliced
1 bunch watercress, washed and dried
1 large onion, finely sliced

In a clean jar, combine all ingredients for the dressing, replace lid and shake well until sugar is dissolved. Set aside.

In a bowl, combine 2 cloves garlic, fish sauce, 1 teaspoon sugar and 1 tablespoon oil. Add steak, mix well and marinate for 1 hour.

Arrange watercress in a salad bowl and toss with a little of the prepared dressing.

Heat remaining 2 tablespoons oil in a large non-stick frying pan or wok. Add onion, ½ teaspoon sugar and remaining clove of garlic. Stir-fry until fragrant. Add meat and marinade and stir-fry for 2 minutes. Serve at once on top of watercress. Can be served with a separate bowl of dipping sauce for added seasoning.
Serves 4.

Wormwood
Artemisia absinthium

Common wormwood grows from a creeping rootstock, sending up stalks to 60 cm with deeply divided leaves. The whole plant is grey-green in colour and covered by fine silky hairs. The small, greenish-yellow flowers grow in clusters on the flower stalks, which need to be cut back after flowering has finished. Tree wormwood (*A. arborescens*), grows to 2 m and has silvery-white leaves.

Grow

Grow new plants of wormwood from seed or root division, both in spring. Tree wormwood is best grown from cuttings. All wormwoods are tough plants and the spreading forms can become problem weeds. They will grow in most soils as long as they have reasonable drainage and will tolerate sun or semi-shade.

Garden talk

Wormwood is not used in cooking but does have medicinal and pest repellent properties. A very weak tea will also aid digestion. Julia calls wormwood *ajenjo* and says it is good for diabetes, wounds and bruises. 'It is useful for many, many things and for many illnesses. I put one of those leaves in water, because it is very, very bitter, but it is very good for your system.' Vilma agrees saying that it is one of the best medicines. 'Just pour boiling water over the leaves and drink it, but it is bitter. ' Wormwood is also strongly antiseptic and a wash made from the leaves can be used to treat wounds, bites and bruising.

Tree wormwood

Zucchini flower

Zucchini
Curcurbita pepo

This annual grows as a vigorous trailing plant with long tendrils, or with short more upright stems to form a bush. It has very large leaves and the whole plant is covered with small prickles making it rough to the touch. Large yellow flowers are followed by long or round fruits that are yellow or green and various combinations of both.

AUSTRALIAN RECIPE FROM ASSI
BAKED ZUCCHINI AND SQUASH

1 medium zucchini, sliced
2 large yellow button squash, sliced
½ onion, finely sliced
½ capsicum, cut into strips
1 clove garlic, crushed
1 teaspoon dried oregano
½ cup fresh parsley, finely chopped
1 tomato, diced
½ teaspoon salt
¼ teaspoon freshly ground black pepper
1 tablespoon olive oil

Preheat oven to 350°F (180°C). In a small baking dish (approximately 18cm x 28cm), place sliced zucchini and squash to cover the base. Next, add a layer of onion, then capsicum and then crushed garlic. Sprinkle with oregano and parsley. Finally, add a layer of tomato. Sprinkle with salt, pepper and oil. Bake uncovered for 30 minutes. **Serves 2.**

CHILEAN RECIPE FROM JULIA
STUFFED ZUCCHINI

6 small zucchini, cut in half crosswise (not lengthwise)
¾ cup soft breadcrumbs
1 cup minced beef
¼ cup uncooked rice
1 tomato, finely diced
1 teaspoon ground cumin
1 teaspoon dried oregano
½ cup parsley, finely chopped
¾ cup water
1 tablespoon olive oil

Using the handle of a teaspoon, scoop out the insides of the zucchini, leaving a solid base. Chop the scooped out pieces finely, squeeze out any excess moisture and reserve the liquid and the flesh, separately. To the squeezed zucchini flesh, add the breadcrumbs, minced beef, rice, tomato and seasonings. Mix well to form a stuffing mixture. Stand the zucchini shells upright in a small saucepan with a tight fitting lid. Stuff each shell with the mixture, pushing down firmly with the handle of the teaspoon. Gently pour reserved zucchini liquid, water and oil into base of saucepan. Replace lid and cook very gently on low heat until tender and rice in stuffing has expanded and cooked, approximately 20–30 minutes. **Serves 2.**

Zucchini

Grow
Zucchinis like plenty of space, good compost-enriched, well-drained soil, full sun and adequate water. Plant seeds where they are to grow from September to early January with about a metre between plants. Top-dress with well-rotted manure at least once during the growing season.

Garden talk
Young zucchinis are baked, steamed, boiled and fried. They are also added to soups, stews, breads and cakes and older fruit go well in soups and can be stuffed. Young leaves and mature male flowers are also eaten. Julia likes to add zucchini to soup with potato and pumpkin. 'Use any vegies you like. An economical soup and very healthy, very thick.' She also stuffs the smaller zucchini, or cuts them in half and puts cheese on top. 'You can cook it in very many different ways, a very useful vegetable.' Hatice also stuffs zucchinis while Georgia likes them roasted or grilled, or baked with other vegetables in a dish called Brium (see page 103). 'A beautiful vegetable dish.'

Further Information

Suppliers and Other Useful Contacts

Some of the suppliers use common names for the plants that are different to the names used in this book. Find them in the catalogues by using the botanical names.

All Rare Herbs
PO Box 91, Mapleton, Qld 4560
(07) 5446 9243, fax (07) 5446 9277
www.allrareherbs.com.au
An extensive range of common and unusual herb plants including aloe vera, edible canna, five-seasons herb (mother of herbs), greater celandine, Chinese boxthorn (Chinese wolfberry), long-leafed coriander, dandelion, fish plant, epazote, gotu kola, perilla, plantain, Vietnamese mint.

Digger's Seeds
105 Latrobe Parade, Dromana, Vic. 3936
(03) 5987 1877, fax (03) 5981 4298
www.diggers.com.au
A extensive range of common vegetable and herb seeds including heritage varieties, as well as snake beans, chicory, unusual chillies, kale, orach, pepino, rocket, alpine strawberry and some more common Asian vegetables.

Eden Seeds
MS 905, Lower Beechmont, Qld 4211
(07) 5533 1107, fax (07) 5533 1108
www.edenseeds.com.au
An extensive range of common vegetable and herb seeds all open-pollinated as well as some Asian vegetables, amaranth, many different chillies, hyacinth bean, dandelion, edible bottle gourd, kale, luffa, Malabar spinach, mallow, molokhia (Egyptian spinach), mugwort, mustard greens, okra, purslane and stem lettuce.

Green Harvest
52/65 Kilcoy Lane, Maleny, Qld 4552
Orders: 1800 681 014
T (07) 5494 4676, F (07) 5494 4674
www.greenharvest.com.au
A good range of common vegetable and herb seeds and plants as well as amaranth, arrowhead, edible canna, chillies, lemon grass, long-leafed coriander, luffa, Malabar spinach, molokhia (Egyptian spinach), mugwort, okra, purslane, rocket and water chestnuts.

New Gippsland Seeds and Bulbs
PO Box 1, Silvan, Vic. 3795
T (03) 9737 9560, F 1800 088 077
www.newgipps.com.au
An extensive range of common vegetable and herb seeds including a large collection of Asian vegetables, amaranth, snake beans, chillies, chicory, cress, edible bottle gourd (New Guinea bean), kale, long-leafed coriander, mustard greens, okra, orach, purslane, shallots, black radish, stem lettuce, alpine strawberry and many different basils.

Seed Savers Network
PO Box 975, Byron Bay, NSW 2481
T (02) 6685 7560, F (02) 6685 6624
www.seedsavers.net

Cultivating Community
PO Box 8, Abbotsford, Vic. 3067
T (03) 9415 6580

For further inquiries and copies of this book, please contact the publisher or the authors:
Penny Woodward, RMB 6715, Balnarring, Vic, 3926
Pam Vardy, PO Box 355, Eltham, Vic. 3095

Internet Sites

http://www.hort.purdue.edu/newcrop/default.html
The Web Site of the Center for New Crops & Plant Products at Purdue University

http://www.newcrops.uq.edu.au/listing/listingindex.html
The Australian New Crops Home Page

http://www.ahs.cqu.edu.au/info/science/pag/AsianVeg/AsianVeg.html
Asian vegetables, Central Queensland University

http://www.rirdc.gov.au/programs/af.html
Rural Industries Research & Development Corporation Asian Foods Research Program

http://www.scs.leeds.ac.uk/pfaf/index.html
Plants for a Future. A Resource and Information Centre for Edible and other useful plants

http://www.recipesource.com
SOAR: The Searchable Online Archive of Recipes.

http://www.ma.iup.edu/Pueblo/latino_cultures/recipes.html
Latin American Recipes – low fat recipes published by the National Cancer Institute, US Department of Health and Social Services (NIH Publication No. 95-3906(s), January 1995)

http://www.ivu.org/recipes
Vegetarian recipes around the world from International Vegetarian Union

http://www.kuali.com/recipes
The Star Online (CyberKuali) from Star Publications, Malaysia

Bibliography

Brissenden, R., *South-East Asian Food,* Penguin Books Australia Ltd, Ringwood, Victoria, 1996.

Chong, E., *The Heritage of Chinese Cooking,* Weldon Russell Pty Ltd, Sydney, 1993.

Creasy, R., *The Edible Asian Garden,* Periplus Editions (HK) Ltd, Boston, Massachusetts, and Singapore, 2000.

Encyclopaedia Britannica Book of the Year, 2004.

Encyclopaedia Britannica, Fifth Edition, Encyclopaedia Britannica Inc., USA, 1990.

Exotic Greens, A selection of Vietnamese herbs, vegetables, recipes and remedies from the Collingwood Community Gardens, Coll-LINK, Abbotsford, Victoria, 1998.

Facciola, S., *Cornucopia II, A Sourcebook of Edible Plants,* Kampong Publications, Vista, California, USA, 1998.

Freeman, M. and Le Van Nhan, *The Vietnamese Cookbook,* Viking Press, Ringwood, Victoria, 1995.

Good Housekeeping Institute, *World Cookery,* Octopus Books Ltd, London, 1972.

Hafner, D., *A Taste of Africa,* Simon & Schuster, Australia, 1993.

Herklots, G. A. C., *Vegetables in South-East Asia,* George Allen & Unwin Ltd, London, 1972.

Hom, K., *The Taste of China,* Pavilion Books Ltd, London, 1990.

Huang Su Huei, *Chinese Cuisine Wei-chuan Cooking Book,* Dept of Home Economics, Wei-chuan Foods Corp., Taipei, Taiwan, 1974.

Huxley, A. (Ed.), *The New Royal Horticultural Society Dictionary of Gardening,* Macmillan Reference Ltd, London, 1999.

Kapsaskis, A., *The Commonsense Greek Cookery Book,* Angus & Robertson, Sydney, 1977.

Lamp, C. and F. Collet, *A Field Guide to Weeds in Australia,* Inkata Press, Melbourne, 1984.

Larkcom, J., *Oriental Vegetables, The Complete Guide for Garden and Kitchen,* John Murray (Publishers) Ltd, London, 1991.

Phillips, R. and Rix, M., *Vegetables,* Pan Macmillan Publishers, London, 1993.

Routhier, N., *The Foods of Vietnam,* Stewart, Tabori & Chang Inc., New York, 1989.

SBS World Guide, 11th Edition, Hardie Grant Books, South Yarra, Victoria, 2003.

Smith, K., *Growing Uncommon Fruits and Vegetables in Australia,* New Holland Publishers Pty Ltd, Frenchs Forest, NSW, Australia, 1998.

Solomon, C., *Encyclopaedia of Asian Food,* Periplus, New York, 1996.

Woodward, P., *Asian Herbs and Vegetables,* Hyland House, Melbourne, 2000.

Woodward, P., *Grow Your Own Herbal Remedies,* Hyland House, Melbourne, 2003.

Woodward, P. *Penny Woodward's Australian Herbal,* Hyland House, Melbourne, 1996.

Yan-kit So, *Yan-kit's Classic Chinese Cookbook,* Dorling Kindersley Limited, London, 1984, 1993.

Index

Page entries in bold indicate the main entry for this person or plant.

Plants

Recipes

Medicinal Uses

antiseptic, 121, 133, 143, 155
anxiety, 114
arthritis, 28, 111, 126, 128, 134

bites, 72, 101, 114, 121, 137, 155
bladder, 134
blood, 95, 111, 120, 121, 126, 128
breath, 106, 134
bronchial problems, 111, 124, 141
bruises, 121, 137, 155
burns, 72

chicken pox, 107
circulation, 111, 126
colds, 113, 114, 126, 133, 136, 141, 143
colic, 102
constipation, 72
coughs, 29, 75, 108, 113, 120, 141, 150
cramps, 107, 124

detoxifying, 101
diabetes, 62, 128, 137, 155

digestion, 94, 102, 123, 133, 134, 155

eyes, 97

fever, 107, 111, 136, 142, 150
flatulence, 105, 142
flu, 113, 114, 136, 150

gout, 134

haemorrhoids, 107
hair, 111, 128
headaches, 75, 114, 142, 150
health improving radish remedy, 141
high blood pressure, 62, 94, 95, 102, 128, 151
hormonal system, 121

itching, 72
immunity, 92, 110

kidneys, 106

lymph system, 121

marigold tincture, 121
memory, 143

nails, 111
nerves, 75

rashes, 72, 107

scurvy, 140
skin, 72, 111, 112, 121
sleep, 75, 124
stings, 72, 114, 137
stomach, 80, 102, 105, 106, 107, 123, 142

tiredness, 95, 114
tonic, 97
toothache, 111

veins, 94

warts, 112
wounds, 72, 121, 155